Upgrade Your
Self-Confidence

Iona Barker

Dedication

This book is dedicated to my younger self and to everyone who's ready to upgrade their self-confidence.

Acknowledgements

Thank you to my clients who inspired me to write this book. Especially those who took part in my Feeling Safe to Be Seen online course, for which I wrote out the bulk of the processes in this book.

To my partner Tyler for all his unwavering unconditional love and support every day. For bringing me snacks, and hugs, making me laugh, and encouraging me as I wrote. Thank you my love for reading it in those final days and helping me edit.

Thank you Ellie who helped me self-publish, for being my sounding-board and voice of reason. Thank you for the laughs, messages, voice notes, and general shenanigans.

To Barbra for supporting me on our Magic Mondays, long may our focus last!

To Anne, Amy, and Megan for giving me the best encouragement, the neuro-spicy pep-talks, the days out, for listening, and for holding space through challenging times as I compiled my thoughts and feelings for this project.

To all those above and the ones I haven't mentioned, YAY for being the best humans, friends, and family I could ever ask for.

Thank you Miss Fynbo (who married, and I don't know your surname now), my Scandinavian English teacher who encouraged me to write for the few months I was in your class. I've written so much since those days (the late 90s), but I finally found the confidence to create a real book like I dreamed about back then.

Finally thank you to writing coach Tina DeMarco for your time, patience, and expertise in helping me get the thoughts out of my head and into this book.

Table of Contents

Introduction

Why do some people seem confident, and some don't?
Why do you feel confident about certain aspects of life more than others?

Self-confidence exists on a spectrum, where we can experience seemingly no, low & insecure self-confidence challenges, to authentic & easy self-confidence.

Self-confidence challenges can look like overcompensation to make up for a perceived lack or weakness in the self by uncomfortably exaggerating or overemphasising a particular trait or behaviour. Self-confidence challenges can be called "low self-confidence" too, where there is also a perceived lack or weakness in oneself. The displays of this challenge can be a fear of being seen, feeling unsafe, inability to act, struggle when putting the self out into the world, and asking for needs to be met.

Authentic self-confidence comes from a secure place of inner trust, alignment with the self, and the way we're living our lives. Authentic self-confidence lights us up. I believe it comes from the core of our consciousness and is a knowingness, relaxed, and secure in the is-ness of its being. It's fun, bold, natural, free, easy, relieving, warm, and gentle. Our authentic self-confidence doesn't need insecurities and feelings of self-doubt. The ego takes a backseat as the true self comes forward because the ego can show as dressed-up insecurities. When we integrate our insecurities, they're no longer in the driver's seat of our psyche. Our true, confident self is.

Our level of self-confidence depends on our upbringing, environment, and experiences. Some people say there are genetics involved too, but I find epigenetics more relevant. Meaning it's all about the experiences, behaviours, and environment that influence who we are, rather than who we're related to.

Our self-confidence challenges can cause us to feel heavy, confused, frustrated, not good enough, powerless, hopeless, helpless, insecure, anxious, depressed, inadequate, guilty, and shameful. All things that perpetuate our stuck-ness in life.

How do we get to the knowingness of our authentic self-confidence? First, we must find out what's going on in our belief system, identify what we're practising at an emotional and mental level, and discover who we are as our authentic, confident selves. Once we develop awareness of the self we can implement practices to re-train our synapses, nervous system, thoughts, and emotions (synapses don't just exist in the brain, we have them in our heart, gut, and other internal organs too). We can learn to relax in our mind, body, spirit, and self.

We all experience different levels of self-confidence along this spectrum, and we're the least confident in the things we feel the most emotional, mental (and sometimes physical) resistance towards. We experience the most confidence in areas of life where we have little to no resistance. Usually, the resistance comes from a belief or perspective of ourselves, our abilities, and the world around us. We're not born with these perspectives, we pick them up from experiences, environments, and other people. They become our learned behaviour and conditioning. For example, being made to feel not good enough over and over creates the belief that we're fundamentally not good enough, which becomes automatic within our nervous system. Our consciousness is then programmed to believe this is our truth. It becomes unconscious. We may not have cognitive awareness that our consciousness finds evidence in our reality and attracts people and circumstances into our life experiences that prove a "truth" to us. We just feel not good enough again and again.

We're usually not even aware of the stories and "truths" that we're perpetuating until we identify them. Awareness is empowerment. Then we can decide what our truth is.

Many practitioners employ a "top-down" approach which looks at cognitive functions and beliefs in the critical-thinking mind. I like to use a mix of "top-down" and "bottom-up" approaches, which use the mind and cognitive functions to identify emotions and feelings in the body (also known as somatic work). The mind, body, and emotions are all one and we cannot keep them compartmentalised. To open up the full being is to invite harmony and coherence to our systems. Those of us who experience self-confidence challenges may not have much experience or practice in this, which is why we start where we can, and take baby steps like we're learning to walk again.

This book is designed to help you upgrade your self-confidence at whatever level it's at, to embody more healthy authentic self-confidence. No matter what level you're at, it will always provide relief from any self-doubt, upgrading your self-confidence to more authenticity, and the profound benefits that come with it.

Just like our electronic devices require upgrades, I believe our inner programming benefits from regular software upgrades.

We're electrical, energetic beings after all.

My self-confidence challenges began in school and followed me in every aspect of my life until one day I decided I'd had enough of it.

I grew up in the southwest of Scotland on the rural outskirts of a quiet market town called Castle Douglas. As a child of the 80s and

90s, before social media and mobile phones, I spent most of my spare time in nature running through the woodlands and fields, or playing and creating in a bedroom I shared with my sister until I was lucky to get my own room as a teen.

My creativity and the outdoors were my therapy. Writing, sewing, drawing, exploring, and dreaming. I was an adventurer at heart, but I was a very quiet child, and often felt lost, like an imposter. I regularly lived in and escaped to my imagination.

I was the eldest of three, and I felt pressure to be the one to do all the things, such as going to college, then university, and living a "successful" life. However, I often struggled with negative critical thoughts, fears, worries, feelings of not being good enough, and like I didn't belong anywhere.

As a sensitive child, and often felt helpless observing the pain of those around me. These feelings followed me through into adult life, but I just put them down as being "part of life". That life was supposed to hurt and be a struggle all the time.

I also felt responsible for the happiness of others while often sacrificing my own. I knew deep down I was different from others around me as I struggled to keep a happy face on and just be "good".

One of the motivators for writing this book was when I recently looked through my memories box where I keep all my school reports. My high school reports said the same thing every term for the 5 years I was there: "Iona needs to speak up more", "Iona is a conscientious student, but she lacks confidence", and "Iona needs more confidence in class". I don't think it ever got spoken about at home. If it did, it probably consisted of "You just need to stand up for yourself and be more assertive". No one ever seemed to have an answer that felt right, and no one ever showed me how to do or be more confident in myself. I wasn't shown how to resolve the conflict within my emotions, or asked why I was constantly escaping the "real world". Everyone around me was busy struggling through their own crises.

In the decade after leaving school, I built up several successful businesses, but I always pushed through the fear and lack of confidence by "faking it until I make it", "feeling the fear and doing it anyway", or overcompensating. Which came across as forced, fake, and unnatural. I felt confident when I felt safe, but that wasn't very often.

From late 2019 to early 2020, I closed most of my businesses as I felt an intuitive pull to take time off and focus on some emotional work. I was fed up with the struggle, there had to be more to life. I'd spent a decade burning myself out for a little "on-paper success", which I hoped would bring me more satisfaction than it did. I ended up feeling just the same emptiness, negative critical thoughts, fears, worries, feelings of not being good enough, and like I didn't belong.

My favourite, and most successful business to date was my creative therapy business called Say It Ain't Sew, which I ran from 2010 to 2019. I facilitated craft classes all over Scotland and the UK to combat social isolation and collective mental health challenges. I loved creating safe spaces for people to come together and talk. I did some counselling training and worked with amazing organisations. However it took a lot to believe in myself and my dreams of the business, and I struggled during the first 5 or so years. There were so many times when no one showed up for groups, or I'd have to haul my kit all around with no money for the bus to get home after classes. During those tough times, I always felt the motivation to keep going. I'd had to be resilient in life due to my experiences growing up, and having tools and the outlet of sewing and creativity helped my own emotional and mental health. I knew it could help other people too.

In 2018 I was feeling like the craft kit and equipment I'd used for so long were a crutch or something that I was hiding behind. Getting in the way of having deep and meaningful conversations with people about what was going on in their lives. I wanted to sit one-on-one with people, really listen, and help them get to the real core of their stress, anxiety, and depression in a way that I couldn't do at that time. I was also getting fed up hauling a heavy kit of craft supplies around the place. So, in 2020 I re-trained in emotional freedom coaching (in 2023 I got some more counselling training to update what I'd received during my work with Say It Ain't Sew) and set up my online business facilitating one-on-one sessions to help people combat feelings of chronic shame, not good enough, anxiety, and uncertainty of the future. These were the core emotions that were relevant to me when building awareness of my self-confidence challenges, and most of the people I was coaching had experienced similar feelings. My clients were telling me stories about their life experiences that were so relatable and very much like what I'd experienced growing up.

In the early days of setting up my new coaching business, my imposter syndrome and self-confidence challenges were at an all-time high. "Who am I to do this kind of work?", "Who in the world is going to want to know what I have to say? I can barely say boo to a goose!", are some of the thoughts that would spiral through my head almost every day. Then there was the concept of charging people for money for my services; I had such low self-worth. All the people around me in my life were struggling financially, and no one seemed to have money to pay for professional help or coaching. Where and how was I going to find the people who could and would pay me? How would I get them to pick me from all the thousands of other practitioners and professionals offering similar services?

Since then, I've done a very deep dive into my self-confidence, my beliefs in myself and abilities, and re-programmed my entire perspectives on business, money, relationships, friendships, and life in general. Using predominantly the processes I'll be explaining in this book.

I could've got by with the level that my confidence was at. I could survive, though I wasn't exactly thriving. I don't believe I'm here to just get by. In childhood I observed most people around me "just getting by" and I knew there must be another way, surely humans aren't here to work, struggle, and barely live?

That little girl who wants to go out there and see all the fun things the world has to offer still exists within me. I'm an adventurer at heart. I believe in the goodness of the world. Now more than ever I feel the earth needs us to be our most authentically feel-good, confident selves. I feel the more I let that little girl come out and play while loving, supporting, and teaching her how to be her fearless, confident self, the safer I feel to be my true fearless self, and the more I want to help others do the same.

I still experience confidence challenges, and I it may be a life-long journey, but I'm here for the expansion, and I'm so much more secure within myself. I now feel like anything is possible. I believe in myself and what I have to offer much more than I used to. I no longer feel pressure to be or do anything to prove my goodness or worth to others, I'm not lost or an imposter anymore. I'm Iona, and I'm here to help humans feel more confident than ever before.

One of my greatest moments of healing was when I learned to trust myself. Self-compassion and self-trust are what I'm all about. I've been on a journey full of ups and downs, but my authentic self-confidence grounded in when I began to trust myself and make confident decisions.

The words from those report cards all those years ago made me feel like there was something wrong with who I was at my core. That my quiet nature was something to be ashamed of. I tried hard to be assertive and "seem" confident, but it felt like a struggle. The truth is, there was never anything wrong with my confidence, I just didn't fit the education system's idea of what confidence "is". I didn't feel safe to be myself there. Instead of being who I wasn't, I began to develop practices that brought more of me out into the world. I learned how to feel safe to be myself.

This book is full of things to do, but let's make it clear that you are indeed a human being, not a human doing.

Your worth isn't determined by your productivity, what and how much you do for other people, what you achieve, or what you produce in your lifetime.

Your worth is certainly not tied to the approval or disapproval of other people.

You're worthy simply because you exist. You're worthy of confidence, joy, money, love, abundance, peace, ease, satisfaction, and anything that your heart desires because you just are.

Contrary to popular belief I don't believe there is an angry bearded man in the sky who is judging us, nor do I believe that it's written in stone anywhere in the universe that we must struggle or sacrifice any part of us to be good enough or worthy. Our beliefs and stories that keep our confidence challenges relevant aren't written on stone tablets anywhere either.

Take a few moments to explore these questions and write down what comes up for you in a notebook or on the notes on your phone.

Questions:

- Where in life do I want to feel and experience more self-confidence?
- If I were to receive a magic wand or a magic lamp that could grant me more self-confidence instantly, how would I feel?
- What would I do with my life?
- What would my days look like? What choices would I make?

(The "magic wand" is a perspective shift coupled with practice and consistency to build & strengthen new neural pathways and connections within the body, a regulated nervous system, and a better quality of life).

We tend to believe that we'll feel better, be better, and have more confidence once we get, do, have, or be the thing we want. This creates a never-ending chase for an elusive self and stuff, and we rarely live in the now. This moment now is really where it's at. This moment now is always where the "magic" happens.

My goal is to get you back into your now moment, where you can live as your most embodied authentic self. Where the old stories and old paradigms that aren't benefiting you or your self-confidence are irrelevant. My wish for you is that you create a new story for yourself, a new paradigm.

You might be familiar with the old paradigm ideas of what self-confidence is. A paradigm that so many of us have been taught, one that we know deep down isn't healthy. The idea that self-confidence means to be too much, too big for our boots, full of ourselves, cocky or arrogant, that no one likes a show-off. Sometimes if we're acting or living from our low or insecure self-confidence, we can feel like others will perceive us in this way. That we'll be judged, rejected, abandoned, cancelled, hated, and that hurts.

I'd like to offer a new paradigm of self-confidence. One that's based on authenticity, compassion, real self-love, energetic sustainability within the self, and a being that, coming from a secure place, knows and trusts itself. A paradigm where a human truly knows who they are, what they want, and what they're available for (and not available for) in life.

Upgraded self-confidence requires exploration, commitment, and consistency, but most of all it requires us to develop trust within and for ourselves.

Keep your promises to yourself by showing up for yourself consistently and doing the processes (the processes are the tools and techniques in this book), but don't give yourself a hard time if you miss a day or two. You'll know internally when you've made a shift and upgraded your self-confidence. You'll know by the way you feel, and how you respond to and feel around others. You'll know when doing things that previously felt scary, and when doing things that you want to do. The shifts are usually micro-shifts, but we can have big ones too.

Take a little bit of time each day to practise one, a few, or all of these processes. It can be as little or as much as a few minutes a day.

You can't mess it up and you can't get it wrong. Mistakes are welcome here.

This is a collection of tools and exercises that I wish I'd been given when I was younger. I hope it helps you as much as it's helped me, and as it continues to help my coaching clients today.

I encourage you to go and get yourself a new notebook plus a pen that feels good to write with. Use the question sections in the book to write out your thoughts and feelings.

This book is not a substitute for one-on-one therapy, coaching, or counselling. It's very much an accompaniment to it, and I highly recommend looking for a practitioner who is right for you to work with. Your emotional and mental health is just as important as your physical health, so it's always worth investing in, and making it a priority, just as much as you would with your body, bones, or muscle. I see emotions as muscles too, we've got to use them to build them. The more we use them, the easier it can be to lift heavy things AKA challenging life experiences.

It's also essential to state that self-confidence challenges could be a symptom of something deeper. It's important to reach out to a medical or mental health professional if you've experienced trauma (PTSD or CPTSD), abuse of any kind (including emotional), neglect, eating disorders, psychosis, or any mental, emotional, and physical health challenges that require immediate attention and relief of symptoms. If you are neurodivergent (ASD, ADHD, ADD, Tourette's, etc), or experience personality disorders, and struggle to feel or name your emotions then speaking with a practitioner to help you identify your emotions and past experiences in a healthy way may be helpful too.

This isn't a medical book, and I can't guarantee results of any kind.

The best way to use this book is to read through it and pick out the parts that resonate the most with you. You may even want to take notes or circle/underline those parts. You have my permission to write in this book! Try out the processes and techniques. Try them all, because you may end up liking or preferring ones that you had a little resistance towards at first. Come back to this book every time you feel like you're due an upgrade, or if you need a little boost of confidence. Use the contents at the beginning and your intuition to guide you to a process that feels relevant for the moment or emotional season you're in.

Don't forget to join me on social media and let me know how your experience with this book is going. I post regular, inspiring content to assist you on your self-confidence journey: I'm @iona_barker_ on Instagram and TikTok, and Iona Barker on YouTube. I also host regular masterclasses, and I have my private coaching practice which you can find out about on my website: www.ionabarker.co.uk
Scan the QR code below for fast access:

Chapter 1

Journalling

Handwriting is a powerful and effective tool for upgrading self-confidence. Regardless of how well you write, you can use the practice of emptying thoughts and feelings onto the page to gain relief and clarity around circumstances and life experiences.

I've been using a diary since childhood, and still have one from my teenage years. I endured situations that resulted in self-confidence challenges, such as being bullied in school, moving from my childhood home, witnessing the breakdown of my parent's marriage, confusion about my feelings, and not having anyone to talk to about or a healthy way to express it all. My diary became my friend and therapist.

I believe keeping this diary helped me to process my thoughts and emotions. It brought clarity to my confusion and assisted me in making confident decisions, therefore helping me feel more confident within myself and my life as a teenager. I feel it saved my mental health and helped me cope at that time. This practice aided me in stepping into a version of myself who believed good things were possible in life, regardless of school, fears, and other challenging circumstances at the time. It also helped me cultivate a passion for writing.

Having a healthy and safe adult to help me unpack and understand my emotions, thoughts, and experiences would have benefited me greatly. Perhaps I wouldn't have faced the difficulties that I did at that time and in later life. I also might not have written this book if I did! However, I didn't have this in childhood, so had to make do with what I had; access to pen and paper.

In my 20s I was introduced to the concept of a daily disciplined writing practice. This practice involved writing every morning after waking up, emptying whatever was on my mind. The idea was to move the everyday thoughts, feelings, and constant mind chatter out of the way so the golden nuggets of my creativity could emerge and play freely.

I found this practice to be very helpful, and I've continued it for almost 2 decades. I certainly noticed a difference in my self-confidence when I hit the paper. I get everything out in what I like to call a "brain drain".

There's scientific evidence of the benefit to our mental and emotional health that handwriting, especially therapeutic writing, has on the brain.

A study by Holden & Mugwera (1) from 2012 here in the UK states that "Indeed we have found that most of a small sample of GPs in St Helens were already suggesting informal writing therapy to some patients. The patients cited that using handwriting was 'enabling them to take control of their own destiny' and 'to allow the patient to clarify and see their thoughts'; especially if the patient volunteers that they find it difficult to express their feelings."

Handwriting triggers the part of the brain used for cognitive functions and grants us access to stored, perhaps long-forgotten memories too. Writing with the hand has superior results compared to using a keyboard. There's evidence the physical action of handwriting reduces stress, anxiety, and symptoms of depression. Especially if we can extract our worries and fears onto the page, it can help us to move through challenging emotions, and circumstances and I believe, feel more confident within the self.

I encourage regular handwriting via journalling with my clients, and what they write doesn't need to make sense. It can be what you did the day before, seemingly trivial thoughts and feelings, worries, fears, lists, and of course, my favourite: giving yourself a pep-talk. The benefits for our mental health are abundant. It doesn't matter how good or bad your handwriting is, it's more about taking the information out of the brain. Getting it out, onto the page, is moving the information and energy from the self, to somewhere it can be observed. Moving it to where it may not seem as difficult or scary as it did when it was stored within the self.

When we're feeling challenged in our confidence, we can experience emotional stress and nervous system dysregulation such as panic, anxiety, anger, emotional numbing, dis-association of our emotional and physical body (also called dissociation), or brain fog combined with feelings of abandonment, rejection, not good enough-ness, unworthiness, shame, sadness, and much more. Writing this out and expressing it by hand can help us move through it and come full circle back to feeling safe within ourselves and our actions once again.

"Tap-In"

Before I do any kind of emotional work I "Tap-in" to my emotional body. I take one or both hands and open the palms up, laying one on top of the other in the centre of my chest. I close my eyes and take a nice deep breath in and out.

Let's try it before we write. Take both hands and place them in the centre of your chest. I like to start with both hands first to create a circuit throughout my mind, body, and emotions before I move my dominant hand away to write with. Make sure your hands are fully open and apply light pressure onto your chest. Notice the texture of your shirt or item of clothing and the texture of your skin on your hands. Now close your eyes and take a nice gentle but deep breath in and out. You may also want to vocally sigh as you exhale, as this sends a signal to your body that it's time to relax. This "Tap-in" process helps switch off our critical thinking mind, so we can access our emotions. With regular practice, you'll notice how beneficial this is. I believe it fosters deep trust for and within ourselves and our being. I find placing a hand on my chest helps me to be honest with myself and others too. To feel more authentically confident, we must learn to be honest with ourselves, our feelings, and with other people.

(This 'Tap-in' process is different from the process of 'Tapping' AKA EFT Emotional Freedom Technique which I'll be explaining further on in the book).

I also teach my clients to "Tap-in" when we're working together to minimise overthinking and to access their emotions more coherently and effectively. I find they have a much more streamlined and efficient session. It also builds up trust within the emotional body of the client, as many of my clients struggle to access emotions and feel they can't trust their own judgment or make decisions. This technique is so great, and I recommend you do it when you're performing any of the processes in this book. It may take some practice especially if you've ever felt unsafe to feel or express your feelings.

In your notebook begin by writing out 2 pages of how your day has gone so far, and how you feel. Write whatever comes to your mind. If you can't think of anything to write about, write about what you can see, hear, smell, taste, or touch in your environment. It may seem weird and trivial at first, and you may look at it and think what a load of nonsense! You don't need to show anyone, and you can keep it somewhere private. This is a practice just for you, to get out of your way. You may struggle to identify and even feel your feelings because it may not feel safe to do so. Can you create a safe space for a few minutes allowing yourself to express and feel your feelings? Maybe you can lie in bed under the covers, close your door, or create a makeshift "do not disturb" sign. Or perhaps you can find somewhere peaceful outside or in nature to do this practice? You deserve to and are worthy of creating a safe space for yourself, and you are worthy and deserving of having that space and time respected by yourself and others.

If you were talking to a friend and loved one about something difficult they had experienced, what would you say to help them feel better? How would you support them?

Try writing to yourself in this way. Write to yourself as if you were a friend and loved one. I do this technique with my clients and their inner child. We'll chat about this a little later though.

Try writing 2 or 3 pages a day for 30 days and watch how it affects how you think and feel about yourself and your circumstances. I'll bet when you look back at what you wrote in those first few days, you may have forgotten all about certain things that were troubling you. Notice how much more confident you feel when you give yourself the space to work through your thoughts and feelings. Writing 3 pages of A4 can be quite a task, so you may want to get yourself a smaller notebook. A5 size or A6 is perfect for this.

I recommended journalling to a client when they were experiencing relationship challenges. They were struggling to communicate their needs to their partner, and I suggested that they use their journal to write out their emotional needs, so they'd be able to communicate more coherently. Using their journal to get everything out first, so that when it came to communicating with their partner, they could be more effective at getting requests for their needs across. They also reported feeling less emotionally volatile and angry when communicating with their partner, as they'd "gotten it all out" in their journal and were no longer "taking their emotions out" on their partner. They saw a positive change in their relationship, and journalling was an opportunity to get to know themselves better too.

Your Self-Confidence Stories

Our self-confidence is based on the stories we tell ourselves about ourselves and our circumstances. These stories can be based on fear, limiting beliefs, and restricting the growth and expansion of our life experiences. These stories could've been projected onto us by others, or by regularly experiencing challenging situations and feelings if we're unable to process and integrate our challenging experiences and emotions in a healthy way.

Let's explore these stories so we can write new ones that fill us with confidence about ourselves, our lives, and our abilities.

Let's ask the question I asked at the start of this book and write it as a heading in your journal or notepad: "Where in life do I want to experience upgraded self-confidence?".

You're going to explore this, expand on what you wrote in the introduction, and write freely to observe without judgement anything that comes up to the surface of the mind.

For example, you could want to experience upgraded self-confidence in work by speaking out more with your ideas, and in your finances by asking for the money that you so rightly deserve. Or perhaps the upgrade is in health by feeling confident in your bathing suit in the pool or feeling confident in the gym? How about relationships and friendships? Like feeling confident to put yourself back out there even though you had your heart broken in the past? Or having the confidence to ask for certain needs to be met by your partner? How about with family members? Such as having the confidence to set boundaries.

Let's be specific here, and genuinely explore the feelings about the situation you desire more self-confidence with. Tap in and take a moment to feel into it. It's safe to feel, and our emotions aren't bad or wrong, they're our guidance system.

Questions:

- What's going on with this situation?
- How do I feel regarding this situation? Powerless? Helpless? Disempowered? Frighted? Scared? In struggle or lack? Is there any fear of rejection or abandonment? Do I feel not good enough in any way?
- What do I believe about myself to experience these emotions and the way this situation is? Do I believe I'm unworthy of what I want in some way because of something that happened in the past? By something that someone said to me, or how they made me feel?

It's important that you not judge anything that comes up, especially if it feels strange or shocking. We're using a gentle curiosity to explore what we've got going on with the stories that we may be playing in our minds at a subconscious level, buried deep in the

7

psyche. When we have subconscious stories (programming) running in the back of our minds, it's like a noisy fridge that hums in the background noise of our home. We get used to the noise and it eventually becomes a part of who we are. That is until we recognise it, pull it out and tell a new story. We give the fridge a service!

Let's look at an example: Say I want to experience upgraded self-confidence with my social media and putting myself out there. What's going on with my situation? Well, when I create content I have a fear that I'm going to get cancelled or trolled at most, or no one sees it and it gets lost by the algorithms at least. I feel unmotivated, disempowered, helpless, and a little bit of not good enough. It feels exhausting spending time creating content that no one sees, and what if no one likes it? What if I get called out for being a fraud, for talking nonsense, or for saying the wrong thing and upsetting people? What if I'm rejected and loads of people unfollow me? What if I get publicly humiliated and people see me as a bad person? When I tap into my feelings around that, it hurts a lot and is frightening.

To experience this, I must believe some things about myself such as I'm worthy of being treated badly, I'm not good enough, and I don't know what I'm doing (even though I have over 13 years experience of supporting humans, over 15 years of running businesses, and loads of training and qualifications). I also feel like I can't trust myself.

My usual behaviour is to give up easily on something as soon as there's any risk of rejection, even when I know what I'm doing has the power to help people. One person's negativity trumps all the positive feedback I get because I can't trust positive people. What if they were lying to me just to shut me up or manipulate me? I grew up with heavily critical people all around me, so it makes sense I trust the critical people more. This was safer for me growing up, it's how I survived. The critical people had all the power, and it was just easier for me to take on their objections than fight them. This has followed me into adulthood where it shows up in so many aspects of my life, especially whenever I attempt to put myself out there... I expect the hordes of naysayers, eye-rollers, and "who do you think you are" crowds with pitchforks.

Take some time and write out as much of your current story as you can, in a similar way to what I did above.

Empty your mind, body, and emotions onto the page, like the brain drain we talked about previously. When you get to a point where you feel like you can't write anymore about it, ask:

Questions:

- How do I prefer to feel about this?
- What benefit is there to keeping this story relevant?
- What would be the worst thing to happen if I were to experience something different and something better?
- Am I available for something different and something better?
- If not, why not?
- What would it be like to experience a different story?
- I get to decide what my truth is, so if I could tell any story and experience anything for myself and my life (no limits), what would it be?
- What's the conclusion of my self-confidence story?
- What's my new story? How does it feel?

Conclude the old story with a new story about yourself and how life gets to be. Now it's your turn to choose a new story every time.

Write this out as your new story. Get specific about how it feels and how you would like it to feel. Tap into and express these new feelings as much as you can right now at this moment.

Continuing with my previous example relating back to my social media and using the questions above, I'd prefer to feel knowledgeable and empowered to use my skills and experience (with the perspective that I don't know all there is to know, and that I'm learning every day). I'd like to feel secure in myself and trust that what I have to say is relevant even if no one sees it. Especially if people see it and don't agree with it. I'd like to stay secure within myself especially when people don't agree with what I have to say. I'd like to not take it personally. I want to feel more confident as a woman and stand in my power more whenever people are sharing opinions that feel triggering. I also understand that I'm not going to be right all the time, and that's okay. Many people would rather prove themselves to be right all the time so much that it negatively affects their happiness and state of being.

Today I had an experience with a local business owner while visiting their shop to use their service. They expressed their opinion to me on gender roles for men and women. It triggered me, and I felt my nervous system's safety responses (dysregulation) kicking in with an adrenaline rush, and increased heart rate, and I wanted to get out of there as soon as possible: My fight, flight, freeze, fawn, flop response.

For most of my life, if I encountered anyone critical of me, especially with such a strong opinion of what, where, and who I should be as a woman, I would've gone into a people-pleasing mode (fawning) and then would have run away as fast as I could (flight) to get myself into a safe place, because my nervous system saw this as high risk.

To experience this, a part of me must believe that they're right, and I'm wrong. That their opinion is the more powerful one, and their opinion has power over me. Or that I'm in danger, I'm powerless, frightened, not important, I don't know what I'm talking about, and the other person (often the man, or sometimes an older person) knows more than me.

It feels yucky and draining. It feels like my age and gender mean that I'm not important (when I'm young I don't know anything, and when I'm older I'm irrelevant). It feels like I'm a victim of a system that's been running for so long, and even though it doesn't truly benefit anyone, I just must accept it because it just "is what it is". This is the story that I was telling myself over and over in my head, perhaps at a level I wasn't conscious of.

This story was my truth for so long, but when I can look at it objectively, I see there are no real reasons why it has to be my fundamental truth forever. I can reclaim my power by deciding something new. I can challenge this story by calling BULL SH*T on it! I know there are people in the world who have different perspectives on this, so why can't I? If I could tell any story about who I am and live it, what would I say? I've met and experienced plenty of people who are older than me but emotionally immature, so age doesn't always mean someone knows more or is more mature. All experiences are valid, and just because my experience is different from another person's, doesn't mean it's wrong. I know and experience so many people (lots of women) who've had to work twice as hard and learn twice as many skills just to be seen and taken seriously for jobs and roles. I've got personal experience of earning less money than my male peers for doing the same job or taking on more responsibilities. I was just supposed to feel grateful for being included or given the work in the first place because if I didn't do it, they'd find someone else who would.

My new self-confidence story is: I'm a confident human being who has a right to, and is worthy of taking up space, a right to feel safe, and supported, and a right to express my own opinion as much as others do. I'm skilled in what I do, in both life experience, and in my business. I'm experienced and skilled enough to know what I'm talking about in everyday life, and on social media, especially when it comes to standing up for what I believe in (I believe in the fundamental goodness of humans, freedom to be/do whatever we want as long as we're not hurting ourselves or others, and I also believe in unconditional love).

I understand that everyone has an opinion, and I can listen, but it doesn't need to affect me. This can be challenging, especially if someone has a strong opposing opinion that has the potential to cause harm to others. I can trust that people are discerning, and I can trust that others can make up their minds. I can give people credit. Everyone is entitled to their opinion, and their opinions don't need to align with mine. It's safe for other people to have different opinions, and it's safe for me to disagree with other people. I know that I'm good at recognising unsafe behaviour or situations (I've been in a few unsafe situations in my life). I know that I wasn't in any real danger during the experience I had today.

I know I want to feel free emotionally, I want to experience inner peace, and I want to bounce back fast when I recognise the triggers (dysregulation), but at the end of the day, I don't want to let this stuff affect me. I want to stop and take a breath. I don't want to feel threatened by it, but it's normal and okay if I do. I want to feel safe, secure, and authentically me. I want to feel certain of myself and my beliefs, and I want to see others (or as many as I can) as fundamentally good at their core, and worthy of their beliefs too. There's enough room in this world for everyone and their beliefs. I know I'm always learning, and if I was to say something that wasn't beneficial for people it would be safe for me to admit a mistake and apologise, keeping myself accountable and willing to see all sides of every story. I know there are people out there who would fight me and disagree with me on all this, and I can accept that too. I have to be alright with people disliking me (this is a tough one for me), there are 8 billion people on the planet. Do I need every single one of them to be my friend?

The conclusion of my self-confidence story is that the old story I was telling myself before wasn't benefiting me at all. It was keeping me limited. Even perhaps stopping me from having difficult conversations. If I can feel curious instead of threatened, then perhaps I can question, to understand why people have such strong opinions on things they do. I don't need to agree with them, but I believe that when we question things, it makes it easier to understand them, to eventually create something more beneficial if we want to.

If I were to go into that situation again, next time with a curious mind, the worst thing that may happen is that person may think I'm agreeing with them, or they may even get defensive and attack me verbally or otherwise. Though as I said before, it's safe for me to respectfully disagree with other people, and if someone is going to be abusive or project their emotions in such a way, well I can get out of there as soon as possible. With the understanding they may have some personal emotional challenges going on. I'm available for respect, kindness, communication, positive experiences, and to listen/be listened to. I'm not available for disrespect, abusive behaviour of any kind, antagonism, trauma-dumping, manipulation, or mind games.

If I were to experience this different story, I would be more fearless in my everyday life. I would show up, stand, and move through the world with more power and much more confidence. I wouldn't hide myself so much. I would no longer be a victim of this system, as I'd be empowered. If I tap into what this feels like at the moment, I stand taller, I breathe deeper and I don't feel frightened anymore. I feel safe to hear different opinions, and I feel safe to express my own (because why would I believe that only some people can have an opinion, and I can't?).

It doesn't mean that I must go out and spend all my time listening to everyone's opinions. I can be selective because, at the end of the day, my time and energy are my most valuable resources. It feels good to be curious, but also mindful of what I say yes and no to, and where I put my energy.

The stories we tell about ourselves, our circumstances, and our lives in general influence every part of us, including how we feel. These stories become our belief system which attracts people, circumstances, and experiences into our lives too. The world needs you to embody and be your new story now more than ever. Calibrate to it regularly. Feel it until it's overflowing from you in every way. This is one of the best ways we can help others too, by standing in our truth. When we become our true selves, the people looking for us can find us.

We upgrade our self-confidence every time we remove the resistance from the areas of life that've felt stuck. We use journalling and the curious exploration of our stories, beliefs, and feelings to bring relief into the mind, body, and emotions. It's safe to think new thoughts, feel new feelings, and believe new stories about us. Nothing is written in stone; our minds are built for change. Human beings are adaptable.

We don't give up our negative feelings or challenging experiences, as these are all part of being human too. We need our "bad" feelings, as part of our emotional guidance system (though our emotions aren't bad or wrong), and when we use practices like this, we can navigate life and all it has for us with more mindfulness, growth, depth, and enthusiasm.

Chapter 2

Meditation & Visualisation

Meditation is sitting quietly for a minimum of 3 minutes regularly to give the brain a rest from thinking. Meditation is a valuable tool for our self-confidence upgrades.

As we spend all our lives thinking, the brain struggles not to think. Many of us get caught up in thoughts and overthinking.

When we practise slowing down our thoughts, we can reduce stress, anxiety, and symptoms of depression, increase our confidence, and manage our thoughts and emotions more effectively.

I'd heard of meditation years before I tried it. I was so apprehensive to try it because the thought of sitting still for any period felt impossible. I was an established fidgeter and over-thinker. I gave it a shot one day when I was just so fed up with my anxiety symptoms.

I agreed to be part of a daily abundance meditation group for 7 days with some friends, and the concept of calming my chaotic mind while becoming more abundant at the same time was attractive.

I sat for 20 minutes each day and listened to the guided meditation recordings, intending to relax my mind and body. During the first few attempts, I struggled to sit still and had to fight a strong urge to pick up my phone and scroll through social media or check my messages. Especially if messages came through during it. I had to set a strict boundary with myself that during the 20 minutes, I only focused on the recording, my breath, and letting my thoughts go. To lean in and focus on feeling relaxed, which felt challenging. It was unpleasant at times because I'd been in mostly flight or fright (freeze, fight, fawn, & flop sometimes too) by overworking, and always moving so that the overwhelming critical self-talk, anxiety, fear, and disappointment with myself and my life was kept at bay. I was also very sensitive to noises and would jump at anything and everything. I was living in my sympathetic nervous system with my body always expecting stressful situations. It didn't feel safe to relax. I had to force myself to relax.

The first few times I tried to meditate I felt the feelings and thoughts of not good enough creeping in, then the fear I was going to miss something, and by sitting still something bad was going to happen. I kept ignoring those thoughts and trying to calm my mind and body by swiping them away. Then the critical self-talk would appear. Things like "This is a waste of time", and "Here's something else that I'll start and fail by giving up, what's the point?". At that time as I was keen for the approval of others, the thought of quitting the 7 days felt bad, and I had a strong urge to prove myself. So every day, despite my harsh thoughts and feelings of anxiety that the world was going to spontaneously combust if I sat still, I pushed on with it. I also started using other techniques to relieve the critical self-talk which I'll discuss later in the book.

By the end of the 7 days, I felt more peace and relief in my mind and body than I ever had before. It was a revelation! It wasn't easy at times, but I felt proud that I'd stuck to the full 7 days, and you know what? I felt more abundant too!

From then I attempted to sit for 20 minutes each day and practise what I'd learned from the recordings: practising letting my thoughts go, focusing on my breath, relaxing my body, and finding stillness among the chaos within my being. I kept a habit tracker on my wall, and I meditated almost every day for a year. Sometimes I couldn't manage the full 20 minutes and would do just 10 or 15 if I had a busy day. I would do it mostly in the mornings, but sometimes I wouldn't have time, so I would try and fit it in some other time in the day. I found that sitting on public transport was a good time to do it, or if I was sitting waiting somewhere. That felt like an effective use of my time and a nice way to feel relaxed in sometimes overwhelming and over-stimulating environments.

After the year was complete I decided to explore other kinds of meditations and that's when I discovered visualisation. I have quite a creative imagination, and visualising was an exciting way for me to exercise channelling the chaos within it, while also quieting my mind. I would do a short visualisation first to set me up for the meditation.

The next year I didn't keep my habit tracker going or manage to meditate as often as before, but it was still a regular practice for me. I saw it as necessary for my nervous system and peace of mind, and it was fun too.

By my third year of regular meditation, I was teaching it to others. I'd been hired by a TV and film production company, and a few third-sector organisations to go in and teach their staff and clients how to meditate. I loved it, and it was so rewarding seeing people's nervous systems, posture, and even their complexions change after doing a short meditation. They stood taller, their faces and eyes shone brighter, and they seemed calmer. It was evidence that meditation gave relief from their overworking thoughts and minds.

I took my meditation classes online for a few years, and gradually fell away from it, both in my practice and in teaching it. I was so busy setting up my current business that I forgot all about meditation. It's so easy to get distracted with thinking and doing, and I was struggling to manage my time. I felt a lot of resistance towards the thought of taking time out of my busy days to sit and do nothing for 10-20 minutes. Ironically, this is the biggest sign that meditation could prove most beneficial to set time aside to cultivate my mental health.

When I feel anxiety creeping into my mind and body, that's the perfect time to sit still and focus on nothing else but my breath. Now I keep a regular practice of quieting my mind and body. I don't do it every day, and sometimes I do it for just a couple of minutes only. It helps me focus, and feel more inner peace and calm, it assists me in staying regulated when stressful things happen in life, and it also allows me to deepen my self-awareness and consciousness of my thoughts and feelings. When I feel triggered, dysregulated, or panicked in my body, I can recognise it instantly. I turn my focus to relaxing instead, because most of the time I'm not really in any danger, but my nervous system thinks I am.

I used to struggle to identify and name my feelings, but regular meditation practice has helped me slowly observe and explore my thoughts and feelings without judgement.

Overall, meditation has helped me to feel more confident within myself. I am relaxed and present. Have you ever spoken to or been around someone who is effortlessly authentically confident? They're usually very relaxed people! It takes a lot to get them riled up or stressed out. Very little phases them, and I feel like they're the natural leaders of the new paradigm. I know a few, and they haven't always felt like this. It takes many years of intention, to choose calm and peace over again. If you ever stop and ask an authentically confident person about their past, they usually have fascinating stories of how they overcame adversity and personal challenges.

In 2023 Forbes published an article called "10 Science-Backed Benefits of Meditation" (2), where they list stress reduction, anxiety management, depression management, lower blood pressure, immune system health, and improved memory as just some of the benefits. I can say I've experienced all these benefits and more. The best thing about meditation is it's free, there's no need for fancy equipment, and you can do it almost anywhere (obviously not if you're driving or doing something that requires focus or attention).

Let's try meditation right now.

Read the following paragraph and then try it for yourself:

Set a timer on your phone or alarm for 3 minutes.

Close your eyes and take a nice deep breath in and out.

With your eyes closed, focus on the sensation of the air coming into your nose and out of your mouth.

What does that sensation feel like? Is it warm or cool? Make a mental note.

What about sounds in your environment? What can you hear?

The goal here is to redirect our focus and attention back to the feeling of the breath coming in and out of the body, or to the sounds in our environment. Both are really good ways of slowing down our thoughts. This is indeed a practice as the brain naturally wants to come back to thinking.

Note: We're not beating up on ourselves if the mind wanders and we start to have thoughts. The practice is becoming aware that it's happening, and then bringing our focus back to the breath or to the sounds in the environment. You may find yourself only being able to focus on your breath or environmental sounds for a second or two. That's great, keep going!

When the alarm sounds, you can get back to your normal doing and thinking.

We're not trying to be monks on a mountaintop or doing it for any reason other than it allows us to relax into an awareness of our consciousness. This'll develop our ability to become aware of and identify the thoughts, feelings, stories, and conversations with the self that keep our self-confidence challenges relevant.

If I'm struggling to pinpoint how I feel about something, or struggling to feel at all, sitting with it in meditation and allowing myself to feel it, after a while (either in meditation or after as I go about my day), it comes up naturally and I shift it effortlessly. I sometimes cry when big feelings come up, but that's ok because crying is the body's way of moving and expressing energy. There's no shame in crying, no matter who you are, how old you are, or what others may say about it. It's healthy. Emotion means energy-in-motion, so when we cry we're actively moving the energy around, and that's exactly what energy does: it moves.

Use your breath to guide you and help you access feelings of relief, gratitude, peace, bliss, love, joy, freedom, satisfaction, and anything else that promotes feelings of well-being. You can also use your breath to guide you through feelings of sadness, guilt, shame, anger, anxiety, panic, and stress. All feelings are valid, and the "negative" ones are just as important to feel for our well-being as the "positive" ones are. Our breath is the most important tool and aid we'll ever use. Without it, we wouldn't last for very long! Try to take long, slow, gentle breaths, filling up your whole lungs, and getting your belly to rise up and down. A nice long breath is nourishing, and satisfying, and sends a message to the brain that you're safe. When we are stressed or anxious, our breath shortens. Many of us who exist in fight, flight, freeze, fawn, or flop during our waking hours can benefit from the practice of deep natural breathing. It's one of the best ways we can come back into coherence and harmony, and for our internal functions and systems to flourish again.

As you practise this technique, you can increase the time on your timer and practice quieting your mind for longer periods.

I love to play with visualisations at the same time as, or at the start of my meditations too.

Visualisations are when we use our mind's eye to imagine or create pictures in our heads of the things we want to happen.

I complete this short practice before any public speaking or situation I feel nervous about. I've also been practising this nearly every day for a few years now. I love it and I find it fun to do!

You may want to try this visualisation before you go into an exam or a job interview.

Sit or stand with your back and neck straight.

Relax your shoulders and body (but especially your shoulders as we hold a lot of tension there).

Imagine you have a ball of light in the centre of your body- between the size of a golf or tennis ball.

Imagine it running up and down the centre of your body in line with your spine.

When you breathe in, the ball of light goes from the base of your spine up to the top of your head, and when you breathe out it goes from the top of your head back down to the base of your spine.

Do this for 30 seconds or so and imagine that it is pulling in all your energy and re-aligning everything back into where it's supposed to be.

On an out breath drop the ball of light out the base of your spine and into the ground (like a trapdoor) and imagine it plugging in with the centre of the planet. (If you like, you can imagine any stories, perspectives, or feelings associated with where you want to experience more self-confidence, being pulled into the ball of light, and transmuted into the earth as it plugs in!).

Once it's plugged in, call it back up into your body, and it brings with it all the yummy, grounded earth energy back into your body.

(I have ADHD so this exercise works especially well for me, as sometimes I feel my energy is high up in the air or outside of me).

With every breath in breathe up the earth's energy into your body and with every out breath, the energy seeps deeper into your being: into your cells and your DNA.

Now after 30 seconds or so with an out breath, imagine the ball of light popping out the top of your head and with it, a fountain of beautiful earth energy spills out and around your body, like a sprinkler!

Continue imagining this and feeling what it might feel like as it washes your energy and body with this energy.

If you can, hold your breath for a few seconds on an in-breath and imagine squeezing the light energy out the top of your head like a fountain.

You might like to imagine connecting the ball light up to the core of the sun, breathing the sun's energy back down into your body- how does it feel to be supported by two powerful planetary bodies of the earth and the sun? The Earth and the Sun are confident in their abilities and selves, so if they could offer you some wisdom, what do you think they would say to you?

This quick exercise helps me to get back into my most authentically confident self. Why don't you give it a go and let me know what happens? How do you feel, and what do you experience? Don't worry if meditation or visualisation doesn't click right away, don't be hard on yourself, make it your own, and have fun with it.

Our bodies rarely know the difference between a real or imagined experience, so visualisations are effective at providing an instant confidence boost.

Our self-confidence upgrades come from within us, never outside of us. We may see or hear something that reminds or inspires us, which can trigger a shift, but the shift must happen within our consciousness.

Even just sitting quietly can prompt a shift, release, some relief, and an upgrade, because we're giving the self and our being space in the moment. We don't need to "do" anything. Sometimes the less we do the better we feel. I'm a big fan of meditation and visualisation because it's free, easy, and innocuous, and anyone can do it almost anywhere (except while driving or operating machinery of course).

Our most profound self-confidence upgrades can be found in the stillness, and sometimes in the understanding that all is well for us and with us in the moment. The most satisfying upgrade of all is the one where we realise, we had it all along!

Chapter 3

Grounding

A human grounded in their being is centred, empowered, certain, relaxed, and responsible. A grounded human is less likely to ignore and suppress their emotions. When we're grounded, we're more aware of the self, and we can face our world with greater ease. Our challenges and apparent stresses seem less frightening and impossible.

Grounding centres us back into our bodies, so we can be our true, authentically confident selves. We can physically ground ourselves by taking our shoes off and walking barefoot on the grass or a sandy beach (though always look where you are walking).

Some studies show the body and our planet as electrical, and when we take our rubber-soled shoes off that act like insulators, we re-create a circuit that benefits our physical, mental, and emotional health. In these studies, grounding is called "Earthing" (3).

We can also ground using our imaginations too. For example, I'm currently sitting in my top-floor flat, and quite far away from the ground. I enjoy grounding myself physically by walking or sitting on the grass in the park with my bare feet, but I also like to practise grounding visualisations too. I believe just like physical grounding helps us, grounding visualisations increase our self-confidence creating coherence, an optimum environment within our system. Therefore relief from the resistance that keeps our self-confidence challenges relevant.

Electrical equipment is safer when grounded to function. Grounding protects our buildings, the occupants within them, and equipment from high-voltage power surges which can be very dangerous without a grounding wire. Excess electricity could surge out of the wiring or equipment and cause damage to people and property. Grounding our homes and appliances means intentionally creating a low-resistance path to the earth for the power to travel. I believe we create a low resistance path for our inner power when we practise grounding. We can drop our resistance to the things in life that we want to experience more confidence in.

Developing a short practice to feel centred in the core of our being, when we've been overthinking in our minds, or feeling anxious or overwhelmed in our bodies is relieving and clarifying. Have you ever felt your energy all over the place? When we ground, we can feel safe to be in our bodies again.

For years I lived inside my head. Things happened that caused me to doubt myself and be on the constant lookout for danger in the form of making mistakes, being criticised, called out, and rejected. It was exhausting. I was walking around so balled up tight and resistant to everything. I began to experience pain in my body regularly starting with aches and pains in my muscles and joints, and then moving all around me. I was in my 20's and having symptoms of someone in their 60's or 70's! It was like my energy couldn't flow around my body, and my power supply was drained or cut off. I was using all my energy to protect myself and keep myself safe from potential risk and rejection. It was like a coat of armour that I'd made myself to stop the "bad stuff" from getting in. It was also stopping me from coming out and being my true authentic, relaxed, happy self. I remember the first times I began playing with "dropping my resistance" and relaxing using grounding. I felt a wave of relief come over my body and I took a huge breath out. I imagined the Earth was enveloping me in her arms and giving me a huge celestial hug of protection. In that place, there is no risk of potential judgement or rejection. At that moment I was safe and relaxed, and I didn't need the coat of armour. Of course, as I was out in the world I felt it creeping back over me, but with time, practice, and intention, the armour has faded and is no longer necessary to keep me safe and secure because I am naturally safe and secure at the core of my being.

The scientific studies on the benefits of physical grounding by walking barefoot on the grass are intriguing. You can even buy special grounding mats to place at your feet when you're working at your desk.

I have a free and fast way that we can ground that's lots of fun to practise.

Let's give it a go!

As you read these words, allow your body to sink into your chair or wherever you are at this moment. Feel your body relax and become heavy. In your mind's eye, see a root system like that of a tree, leave the soles of your feet, and enter the ground beneath you.

Imagine the root system, like a wise oak tree, is travelling down through the floors and walls, into the foundations and earth.

Your root system is now winding and growing in length to 5 metres into the ground, and then 10, 20, 50, 100 metres into the ground! How far into the ground can it go? Can it stretch to the centre of the planet?

Let it effortlessly pass by any pipes, cables, and underground transport systems.

When you've reached your preferred depth into the ground, imagine you're now breathing up the rich, abundant energy into your root system and travelling back up through the ground towards you. If you were to give it a colour, what would it be?

It's now at the soles of your feet, and with every breath, it travels up through your legs, hips, and into your torso.

With every breath out you can feel it surge up into your heart, lungs, muscles, and bones. It energises every cell in the body.

As you breathe in, it fills up your whole being and flows out of the top of your head like a fountain.

Let it wash over you for a moment and enjoy the feeling that it gives you. How do you feel?

If you like, call your root system back into your body, or if you wish, you can leave it "hanging out" in the ground. I leave mine embedded so I can "plug in" to the earth much quicker the next time I do it.

Play with tethering yourself to the ground while you're on a train, a bus, or even on a plane. Do you feel any different or is it the same feeling?

Don't worry if this exercise feels strange or like nothing is happening. When we try new things, it doesn't mean we're bad or we can't do it, it just means we're new to it. Try again a few more times perhaps throughout your day or once a day for a week and see if you can feel the difference in your mind and body.

When I do this exercise with my clients, I often ask them how confident they feel on completion. They tell me how much their posture has changed, how much more centred and relaxed they feel, and of course, how much more confident they feel within their self and being.

Grounding can prompt micro upgrades to your self-confidence. It can also give you a healthy boost if you're feeling nervous about a task, such as having difficult conversations with another, or a group of people. It relieves the resistance just like the grounding in your home and electronics. With regular practice, grounding your mind, body, and emotions can lift the resistance from you too, calling back your energy and permitting your power to flow freely. Your body is a very powerful machine, and any confidence challenges can be transformed by removing the resistance and allowing the flow of energy to return.

Chapter 4

Verbal Ventilation

Verbal ventilation is speaking from your feelings that relieves and resolves emotional stress.

When we're feeling challenged in self-confidence, we're usually experiencing core emotions and perspectives that exist deep within us, such as grief, sadness, abandonment, fear, rejection, loss, not good enough, lack, etc.

Just like handwriting, speaking this out to someone who can see us, validate those feelings, and listen to us without judging them or trying to fix/solve them is so powerful.

Our feelings are not bad or wrong, they exist as our guidance system. When we suppress, depress, or repress them, we're keeping them within us. When we feel them, sit with them in meditation, write them, and speak them out, they can dissipate from the body, and we can create relief around the heavy challenging emotions and stories that we've perhaps been carrying for decades.

Holding on to our experiences and not expressing them for fear of being rejected, shamed, or a burden, can negatively affect our self-confidence. We no longer feel safe to be ourselves, express ourselves and say how we feel. We retract, keep ourselves small, and become people pleasers, living in fear of being called out, told we're wrong, or fear making others feel bad.

Like when we use journalling to express our thoughts and feelings, we're moving the energy out from our body and onto the page. When we manage our venting to one or two pages, we have a set amount of time and space to get it out. Once it's out it's out, and perhaps easier to see from a fresh perspective.

We don't want to spend all day overthinking it and festering on it. This isn't a beneficial use of our time or energy. Often, whatever we write doesn't seem as scary or heavy on the page as when we were holding it within us. We can be objective about it and see it differently. We then have the power to change our minds (thoughts and feelings) around it. It's the same when we verbally vent. If we have a safe, non-judgmental person we can vent to for an allocated time, we can feel seen and heard, validated in our thoughts and feelings, and then have a different perspective offered if we require it. We don't want to bombard this person with hours of ranting and complaining, because that won't feel good for either person. Asking a non-judgmental, pragmatic, objective person to sit while we vent for five to ten minutes can be very helpful in processing our thoughts and emotions.

Think of it as speaking your emotional truth. Perhaps you did this in the past and were condemned or punished for it. This is why it's important to verbally vent to someone who is not going to judge you. You must find a human who is going to listen without giving a solution if you don't want it. Sometimes all we want is to be heard and seen and allowed to feel what we feel. Occasionally this is enough to move us through the difficult feelings. When we vent to another, we must keep the topic on ourselves, and never go into blaming, shaming, or taking it out on the person who is listening to us. As soon as we shift into aggressive, antagonistic, or toxic behaviour, the person we're communicating with will most likely want to get as far away as possible, and they'll go into a defensive mode. Maintaining an element of mindfulness when we vent to others is helpful.

When we allow ourselves to vent regularly, we're coming back to our emotional truth again. We're remembering who we are and that it's healthy and okay to express how we feel. Our feelings are valid, even if they don't make sense to other people. Especially if we've been triggered by someone else's behaviour or words. It can bring up something we experienced in the past where we felt unsafe, and our emotional needs or requests for needs weren't being met. Upgraded self-confidence is all about identifying our needs, requesting our needs, and meeting our needs.

Many of the difficult things we've experienced were not our fault, but it is our responsibility to transform it all, so we can release the past that's keeping us feeling stuck, frustrated, or not good enough.

Neuroscience in children shows that a developing brain needs certain emotional and physical aspects from their caregivers such as loving physical contact, emotional validation, healthy attention around challenging or confusing emotions and experiences, understanding, and emotional safety. Without these things brain chemistry can under develop, forming mental, physical, and emotional challenges in adult life (4).

When we express our thoughts and feelings to other people (not going into blaming or condemning that person), and they have a problem with it or deny/ignore it, it can reflect that other person's emotional intelligence and maturity. They perhaps weren't allowed to express how they feel at some point in their lives and seeing you do it reminds them of how bad they were made to feel. The emotional pain is too much for them. This is never a good reason for us to deny verbally ventilating. It just means that we need to look elsewhere for someone safer, more emotionally mature, and more available to hear us. Crying is not immature, it's a healthy way to express energy that's built up in the body. Stopping yourself and others from crying is blocking and compounding the energy that's trying to move. Remember that emotion means energy in motion.

Not all humans and adults are safe to vent to. It's important to find humans who can be objective and still while you express your feelings, without adding their opinions or advice. It's especially vital to find those who don't shame, dismiss, blame, project, reject, or deny your emotions or reality. Maybe you can't think of anyone who can do this for you right now. You're worthy of being seen and heard while you feel the full spectrum of your emotions and healthily express them. The purpose of this is to feel better, not worse. If you catch yourself shaming or berating yourself for the way you feel or for talking about your experience or feelings, that's not what venting is for. You can express your shame and how you feel, but punishing or emotionally abusing yourself is not healthy or kind.

It's also helpful to be aware of our venting and existing in these painful conversations for the sake of it. Many of us grew up in environments where complaining, bitching, and negativity was part of the family culture. We may have picked it up and got involved in jibes and jabs of others so we could feel included and accepted. Negatively talking about others, especially when they're not there to defend themselves isn't healthy or beneficial for anyone. Have you ever witnessed someone you know speak harshly of a mutual friend who isn't there, then wonder what they're saying about you when you're not around? People who are authentically confident rarely feel the need to bring other people down in any way. In my experience, it's the opposite.

Authentically confident people uplift and support others no matter if they're in the room or not. Authentically confident people are empathetic, kind, and self-aware.

It's also helpful to be objective of those we seek counsel from. We're not judging, but we're unlikely to be seen, heard, and validated by anyone who cannot see, hear, and validate themselves. For example, would you take relationship advice from someone who keeps attracting abusive or unsuitable partners? We must be aware of who we can vent to and ask for advice, and not take advice from those whose lives we wouldn't necessarily want. This is helpful to remember if you ever received criticism from someone who is in no place to give it.

Judgement can come from places of lack, jealousy, insecurity, fear, and sometimes even boredom.

This is why it's very helpful to see a practitioner like a counsellor, coach, or therapist so you can vent. These people are professionally trained to listen. We pay them to listen.

The difference between a coach, counsellor, and therapist is that a therapist is usually medically trained in several practices that focus on psychology, psychiatry, psychotherapy, mental health, and more serious challenges humans might have with their mental health, emotions, and personality. Therapists can psycho-educate us on the science of why we feel the way we do and guide us towards relief of our symptoms and further support. In the USA a license to practise and treat mental health conditions must be obtained before becoming a therapist. Therapists usually have further education such as post-graduate, master's, or doctorate.

A counsellor has similar training to a therapist and may specialise in a particular aspect of mental health or a specific style of practice. Counsellors can work in the community more, like in a school, church, or third-sector organisation like a refuge, charity, or volunteer clinic. Counsellors can have similar or less training than therapists, and they tend to not treat serious mental, emotional, and personality challenges. Some counsellors are trained through their jobs and may have started in a different industry, re-training in later life.

Coaches guide us to specific practices and help us move into a more self-sustaining lifestyle. Coaches can be trained, but some aren't. Many coaches such as life coaches use their life experience and knowledge of how the world works to help others. Coaches specialise in specific areas of life and business, and many are not trauma-informed or able to identify more serious challenges to mental, emotional, or physical health. Unless they have a speciality or niche expertise in an area of mental, emotional, or physical health, that's not the role of a coach. A coach takes what we have and pushes us forward.

I see therapists and counsellors as helping us move the heavy stuff out of the way so that coaches can help us bring the lighter stuff in. They all do different things and they're all relevant and beneficial to helping us transform our inner and outer paradigms.

Therapists can be counsellors and coaches, and coaches can be counsellors who have the training required but might prefer to focus on coaching their clients. All are meant to provide support and space for us to explore our thoughts, feelings, and experiences. They're all different and all very important in how they assist us. They all differ in quality and ability, for example, you may find a coach who has 15 years of experience in your chosen field or aspects you want to work on a better fit for you than a therapist who doesn't know about that topic. Some therapists, counsellors, and coaches are licensed and certified, yet don't practise what they preach. Creating a "do as I say, not as I do" kind of energy. This can be confusing and conflicting for their clients.

It's very powerful, especially if we've experienced relational trauma, to have someone sit with us as we do the work. It's not the job of the practitioner to fix us or give us all the answers, though they may offer wisdom and different perspectives. They're here to view our situations (hopefully) objectively and compassionately with different levels of awareness. It's worth investing the time to find a practitioner who is right for you and what you need, depending on your circumstances and situation.

I saw a tremendous difference in my inner dialogue once I began receiving support from a practitioner. Even just knowing I could sit and let my feelings and thoughts out in the open and not be judged for them was relieving. It took me a while to find an experienced practitioner who could hold space for me while I processed, but I'm so glad I persisted. I felt seen and understood for the first time in my life. Many people (and practitioners) I vented to in the past would often cut me off mid-sentence, interject with their own opinions, disagree, or just dismiss it all completely with invalidating phrases like "it's not like that at all", "life is hard", "get over it", "you'll be fine", "It'll be fine", and my own personal favourite: "that's just how it is", ("it" being life, a person, a thing, or an experience).

When someone could empathise with me and see how and why I felt the way I do or witness the thoughts I was having in my mind without telling me I was "crazy", was a revelation. I often felt guilty for venting to friends and family, like I was adding to their pile of struggle by expressing my own. I felt like a chronic complainer, or a pest, even though I was going through some of the biggest challenges of my life. I now realise these people didn't have the capacity or the insight to support me in the way I needed it. They were just trying to get by too, going through their tough moments and life challenges.

It took me much courage to muster up the confidence to ask for help, or for a moment to express myself, that it was so disheartening to be met with an invalidating phrase or dismissive behaviour. I realised the people I was seeking counsel from were fighting their own battles, so no wonder they dismissed me with invalidating phrases and behaviours. It had nothing to do with my own experiences, and it wasn't because I was too much, which I often thought it was. It was because they often had very few boundaries and would take my stress onto their pile to carry when that's not what I needed.

Many years ago, something in me knew that my thoughts and feelings needed to be expressed, so I began working with practitioners, who were very supportive, but quite limited in their abilities to listen and validate. I worked with my first few coaches for several months but felt like I couldn't freely express how I truly felt during the sessions. I felt it was bad or wrong (shame), and I still carried a huge fear of rejection. I needed the coach to tell me that I was doing a good job. I needed their approval, and I needed to prove to them I was good and have them tell me I was good, even though I wasn't getting to the crux of my challenges.

The people I hired were also not as trauma-informed as I needed, which is fine if I didn't have any underlying experiences or circumstances that were affecting my everyday moments. I was carrying a great deal of trauma from my childhood and adolescence that needed addressing. It wasn't simply just a case of "shifting my perspectives", as many coaches and practitioners I worked with focused on. So I sought the help of practitioners who understood the relationship between thoughts and feelings. I looked for ones that were comfortable with me talking about heavy stuff. I looked for ones that offered me an approach that felt right. I tried a few different ones until I found one that I felt safe being myself around, and who could challenge my detrimental thoughts and feelings. One that I

38

could vent to who wouldn't judge or shame me, but would help me become aware of what I was experiencing and offer me clarity.

Many of us have decades of challenging experiences that have not been processed in a healthy way, so working with a practitioner can be a long process. The relief, inner peace, and increased self-confidence can appear much faster when we work with others than they would on our own.

However, you can also try venting to yourself out loud, which may seem silly at first but notice if it helps you to move through your experiences and emotions in a healthy way. Can you identify how you feel in this moment right now and proclaim it out loud? "I FEEL...". Well done! You just verbally ventilated. That feeling isn't bad or wrong, it just is. We don't need to judge it either.

Lots of people are emotionally stuck at age they experienced challenging or frightening circumstances. You can see this when you're experiencing an adult behaving like an angry child. It's important not to judge others when we observe this, but to accept them for their emotional limitations and resistance.

The best way we can help others is to help ourselves first.

The only way we can ever influence people is by becoming emotionally responsible. By developing our most authentically self-confident, grounded, secure selves.

Many of us experience the challenges we do because we didn't have a safe space to express and move through our emotions, fears, doubts, and challenging circumstances (trauma) in a healthy way when we were younger. When our brains and bodies were growing and developing.

It's never too late, as our bodies are designed to learn and change at any age.

Beginning and cultivating a practice of verbal ventilation can help you develop inner trust, dropping the baggage of life that keeps you from living as your authentically confident self. Taking control of your emotional health through regular verbal ventilation, being seen and heard in our experiences in a non-judgmental way, can profoundly upgrade self-confidence.

Chapter 5

Confidence Credit Score

If you can imagine your self-confidence as a credit score system, how low or high would it be daily? Imagine your capacity to get jobs, make money, form loving and fun relationships and friendships, manage your physical, emotional, and mental health was based on your confidence credit score. You don't need to do anything to increase your credit score. You're already good enough to have and be all the things you want. It's all about transforming your perspective of yourself.

Let's give your confidence credit score a big boost:

In your journal or notebook write the headings and list:

- My accomplishments in life so far

Our accomplishments can be things such as re-organising something so that it works better, crossing something off the to-do list, identifying, and solving problems.

Have you ever put lots of work into something creative, personal, familial, or professional and had it turn out better than you ever expected? Sometimes even getting out of bed, cooking a meal, or doing the laundry can be an accomplishment. If writing a list from your whole life seems too much, then what have you accomplished today, this week, this month, or this year?

- My positive personality and physical traits

If you could look at yourself through the eyes of another person, what would you see? If you saw yourself as a friend or loved one, and this person needed your love and support you would most likely offer it, right? If you were to give this friend or loved one a pep-talk, what would you say? You would complement the wonderful aspects of their personality and then perhaps their beautiful physical traits too. For example, you're thoughtful and conscientious, and you have beautiful eyes! What else would you say about this friend or loved one? This loved one is you! Thinking good things about ourselves can be a struggle and a bit cringe, especially if we've grown to dislike ourselves. Many of us were raised to believe that liking ourselves is selfish, conceited, or narcissistic. Any attempt to build ourselves up will create resistance. That's why I practice viewing the self from another perspective. As if the self was a loved one or friend that needed our love and support.

- Good deeds done

Even though you may feel not good enough at times, I believe you've done a lot of good in the world. Can you think of good deeds you've done for other people in the last week, month, year, or decade, especially if you didn't ask for or get anything in return (unconditionally)? If you haven't done anything you can think of, is there anything you'd like to do for others if you could?

- My peak life experiences so far

What have been the most favourite moments in your life so far? One of mine was lying on a beach in Spain with my partner looking up at the stars. Another of my peak moments was getting my first two coaching clients on the very same day! Tap-in and recall all of the fun and satisfying times in life.

- Things in life I enjoy

What do you love to do in life? What simple things satisfy you? What interests you? What gets you excited? I love flying, travelling, exploring new places, relaxing, being creative, and having expansive conversations about ideas and possibilities of life and the world. I enjoy tasty food, crisp autumn days, and warm summer nights. I love the sunshine and appreciate nature. If you could do anything in the world, where money and time were of no consequence, what would you do?

- Good intentions in life

What are your intentions in life? Perhaps you had intentions when you were younger? Have your intentions changed or are they the same? For example, I intend to live a long, happy, peaceful life. I live intending to create a happy and nurturing environment so I can grow, and help others grow too. I intend to be more of my true self every day, and I intend to do what lights me up. I intend to be creative always and never force it. I intend to lean into the seasons of my life and go with the flow.

- My values

What do you value in life, yourself, and in others? For example, I value kindness, trust, honesty, creativity, connection, altruism, faith, respect, courtesy, fearlessness, compassion, love, patience, freedom, peace, understanding, tolerance, health, courage, authenticity, and grace. You may think of many I haven't written here because everyone's values can be different.

- My good habits

Our habits are the large and small things we do all the time that make up our lives and behaviours. Our "good" habits are the habits that are beneficial and don't harm us or others. Our good habits are the actions and behaviours that can be subconscious too, as in, we've forgotten to think about doing it. We do it on autopilot. What good habits do you practise regularly? One of my habits I class as "good" is not crossing my hands or arms on the steering wheel when I drive. It's a habit I picked up when I learned to drive 20 years ago, and it stuck with me ever since. For example, you may regularly check in with a friend, or avoid certain foods. Anything you do consistently to help you feel better, more aligned, more productive, and more content in your current moments or long-term is good enough.

- What was I like in childhood?

If you were to view your childhood self now, what would you see? What positive aspects does this child have? Are they creative, excited, optimistic, patient, caring, playful, fun-loving, animal-loving, or bubbly? Perhaps they are fearless or assertive? What else are they like?

- Celebrations in my childhood/adolescence

Did you experience anything in childhood or adolescence that felt good? Maybe you won a race on the school sports day, or your teacher showed your work in front of the class as an example of what to do. (Note that it may be challenging to remember back to school, especially if we experienced struggle or difficult experiences at that time). Perhaps you remember spending time with a kind person, or having a favourite toy or special occasion? Our intention here is to remember the good times and celebrations.

- Obstacles I overcame in my life so far

By now in this exercise, you most likely have had a few negative experiences pop into your mind while looking for the positive ones. Let's use this last point in the confidence credit score system to address these experiences and turn some of them into obstacles that you overcame. Of the not-so-good times that popped into your mind, what ones have you overcome? Give yourself the "credit" for setting boundaries, removing yourself from detrimental situations, relationships, friendships, and interactions, and prioritising your health.

When you look over the results of your confidence credit score, how do you feel? Does it increase confidence? You can use the results of your confidence credit score when you experience negative inner dialogue. I call this the inner critic, and sometimes it chimes in and puts us down. This can happen when we think back to a tough time, or when we're feeling triggered emotionally. I'll be talking about the inner critic in more depth later. You can use the confidence credit score to feel better if you experience external criticism from others because even though it hurts, criticism is rarely about us and what we've done or not done.

Some people who witness us feel threatened by us, either consciously or subconsciously, and try to make us feel bad so they can feel better. They might not even realise they're doing it. You might have experienced this if you ever hyped yourself up for something. You went out into the world with a spring in your step, only to be shut down, minimised, and made to feel not good enough once again. This is why it's so important we work on building a secure and steady base to exist.

We must recognise that our self-confidence can't rely on external validation or the opinion of others. It's energetically unsustainable for us to be or do what other people want us to be or do. We can't build a solid foundation on a swamp. This is what it's like to always be relying on others to build us up, to give us our approval, and to determine our worth. It's a swampy inconsistency full of crocs and alligators lurking in the background ready to take our energy and use it as their own.

Crocs be-gone I say!

Chapter 6

The Availability Game

One of my favourite tools I teach my clients for greater self-confidence is helping them decide what they're available and not available for.

What are you not available for in work, relationships, friendships, family, finances, health, and life in general?

In your notebook, write the phrase "I'm not available for", and then underneath, write down some things that you're not available for.

Here are some things that I'm personally not available for, and you might not be either:

- Disrespectful behaviour

Disrespect can look like aggression, animosity, anger, rudeness, insults, uncivil words, and behaviour. I would class any projection of hate, offensiveness, or negative emotion onto another as disrespectful. When we experience consistent disrespect, it eats away at our inner reality, causing us anxiety, shame, and even things like fatigue and depression.

- Lateness

Time is one of our most valuable resources. If we or other people regularly can't keep appointments or meeting times with us, like disrespect, we're just not available for it. Lateness damages our relationships, effectiveness, and even profitability in our businesses.

It can have a knock-on effect for the rest of our day and can create more stress and workload in the long run.

- Criticism

There's a difference between helpful feedback and criticism that feels bad. Criticism can be personal and include jabs or jibes about appearance, personality, ability, or something we've done or not done. Criticism usually comes from the disapproval of another, highlighting a perceived personal flaw, mistake, or fault. We all have flaws and faults (it's safe to make mistakes), but constantly bringing our awareness to them is painful and wears away our self-confidence. If we're around people who regularly point out mistakes or misgivings, they may think they're doing us a favour or helping us by "being realistic", but it emotionally hurts and is more detrimental than beneficial. They may be projecting their fear, shame, lack, and doubt onto us. We're not available for that.

- Going under a certain amount of money in bank accounts

If your month is longer than your money sustains, setting an intention that you're not available for going below a certain amount of money can help keep healthy spending habits. Maybe you're no longer available for dipping into your overdraft? Practise deciding what you're available and not available for with your finances when you're out and about, and you might find yourself less likely to lose track of your spending. This is especially helpful if you feel like you're constantly chasing your tail, and never have any money left over to do the things you want to do.

- Working after a certain time of day

Another time boundary! Our time is an asset, one that we spend, so we must be aware of where we're investing it. Especially when it comes to work-life balance (being a stay-at-home parent also counts as work here). Will you look back on your life and be glad you spent all that extra time at the office or doing laundry? Think back to the values that you set for your confidence credit score, do your values match up to your work life? If you value your leisure time but are sacrificing it for hours at work, maybe it's time to revisit those values and bring them into your working experience. You never know, they might benefit your job and employment, and you may end up being in a better position too.

- Working through break time

Most of us do well with short breaks often. Not taking breaks can affect our productivity and self-confidence. Setting a healthy boundary with how much we're working, and how much rest we're giving our brain and body will help us to say no when others ask us to sacrifice our time and health for them and their projects. You don't owe anyone anything outside of your allocated working hours unless it's agreed in your contract. I've always had a problem with homework from school (sorry teachers!). Expecting children to work outside allocated school time in their home and rest time teaches them poor boundaries, to sacrifice themselves, ignore their own needs for rest and recovery, meet unattainable and unrealistic expectations, seek approval of others, and develop fear and lack-based obedience.

- Not getting outside for a walk and fresh air all-day

Prioritising self-care and practices that help us feel better will increase our self-confidence. How much do you prioritise healthy practices such as getting outside in fresh air for a walk? What about exercise in general? Moving our bodies is so helpful in increasing our self-confidence, and a walk in nature can ground us, bringing us back to our centres.

What other things can you think of that you are personally not available for that I haven't mentioned? List these out in a notebook or the notes on your phone.

Next, write the phrase "I'm available for" and then list what you are available for in similar aspects.

Some things that you might be available for could be:

- Positive experiences

Perhaps you grew up in a home that didn't have many happy times, or you've experienced hard times in your life. What would life look and feel like if you let more fun times in? What kinds of positive experiences would you like to have?

- Fun, loving relationships.

I believe all humans are worthy and deserving of fun, loving relationships. Whether that's friendships, family, or romance. What would life be like if you experienced more fun, loving interactions with other human beings? What kinds of experiences and people can you see happening? What would you like to experience?

- Compliments

It feels great to give someone a heartfelt compliment, like when we give a positive comment on a piece of clothing or a new haircut. Why do so many of us struggle to receive them? Perhaps we think there's an ulterior motive, or we must counter their compliment with "This old thing?" to appear grounded and not too full of ourselves. What would it be like to feel safe to receive sincere, genuine compliments?

- Respect

When we treat others with respect we're indirectly saying, "You deserve to be here, you deserve to take up space, you deserve to be seen". We have a regard for their rights, feelings, and wishes. When we're available for respect, we're available to have our rights met as human beings. Respect is "I'm okay with you and I'm okay with me". We don't need to agree with people to respect them. When we're available for respect, we stand in our power. We're commanding positively, not assertively or aggressively. It's energetically freeing.

- Kindness

Kindness is the consideration of thoughts, feelings, and needs. It's a selfless way of being that I associate with lightness, ease, and warmth. When someone is kind they put us at ease, and it's a positive and loving experience. What does it feel like to be kind to others? What does it feel like when others are kind to you? Can you create a healthy expectancy for kindness?

- Getting places at just the right time

If time is an asset and resource, and we're available for spending and investing just the right amount, what would it be like to be everywhere we're supposed to be at the exact right time? Remember we're a product of the stories we tell ourselves, so can we tell a new story about our timekeeping and act in alignment with it? Being late (and even being early) can create anxiety, so what if we remove the possibility of anxiety and decide we are available to be everywhere just on time?

- Feeling good about looks

We all have things that we'd like to change about ourselves, and many of us want to experience what we don't have. For example, when I was a teenager I was very slim, and often told I was "too skinny". I wanted to experience what it would be like to have curves, and in my 20's my weight increased. I then felt very self-conscious about my body weight and being "too big", so I worked very hard at getting back to that same weight from my teens. It was impossible, as my body changed with age, I was putting so much unhealthy pressure on myself to be "acceptable". I was often emotionally beating up on myself for not being good enough, skinny enough, pretty enough, etc. When everything is relative, it's up to me to decide for myself what's good enough, pretty, and acceptable with unconditional love and kindness. I started exploring the concept of loving and appreciating the shape of my body, and everything that my body does for me, no matter what size it is. I used to be anxious for the approval of my body when all that mattered was my approval.

- Earning more money this month

Money DOES grow on trees (It's made from paper & plants!). I also believe that money doesn't just need to come from your pay cheque or your partner. There's an infinite number of ways that money can come to you. For example, you could find some on the street, get a surprise tax rebate, be gifted it from a long-lost family member, win a prize, sell that box of clutter at the back of the wardrobe online, and much more. When we become available for abundance, we're no longer restricted to money coming to us in the ways we've only known it to. Are you available for abundance and overflow of money?

- Having difficult conversations with people if it benefits

It takes courage to have tough conversations, but communication is valuable, and to get our needs met or experience the relief we require, we sometimes must have seemingly difficult conversations with people. This isn't about going around bluntly telling people what we think of them, it's lovingly and respectfully communicating with people what we prefer and need.

What other things are you now available for in life? I like to start with what I'm not available for because I find it easier to decide what I do want after knowing what I don't want. You can even look at each list and bring the opposite of that aspect onto the other list. My clients regularly tell me how much this changed their daily life experience and increased their self-confidence too.

Many of us go about our day-to-day lives without having boundaries in place. Practising this daily is boundary-setting for yourself and others. It may also help you to say no to things that you might not feel confident saying no to. You can simply say "I'm not available for that". Keeping boundaries is one of the most important forms of self-care. Many of us were trained and programmed to be self-sacrificing, giving up our own needs and wants for those of others. This isn't authentic self-confidence. An authentically confident human stands in their power and conviction to communicate what they will and won't accept. This process is a great way for us to upgrade our self-confidence to get grounded in our boundaries.

What does a crossed boundary feel like inside of the body, and how can we respond in a loving way to ourselves?

Boundaries

A boundary is a material, physical, mental, time, energy, and emotional line that we make to ensure our physical, mental, and emotional safety and protection of our resources. A boundary is not an expectation that we project on other people or ourselves.

For example:

Material boundaries protect our possessions.

Physical boundaries keep our bodies safe against things like proximity, touch, and unwanted comments about our physical body or appearance.

Mental boundaries ensure our thoughts, beliefs, values, and opinions are respected.

Time boundaries guard our time resources and availability.

Energy boundaries ensure we're not over-investing energy or spending it on things that aren't beneficial for us.

Emotional boundaries guard our emotional health against things like trauma dumping, emotional abuse, rejection, and inappropriate questions or over-sharing.

We must be able to develop and respect our boundaries, and it's not anyone else's job to uphold our boundaries for us. Especially if we spent time around people who practiced poor boundaries. We may not know how to create or keep a boundary. It can feel very uncomfortable to put one in place. Which is why I love the availability game. Every time we feel the need to set a boundary, but are unsure or uneasy, we can cross-check and refer to what we're available and not available for in life. If we're not available for disrespectful behaviour and we experience a disrespectful interaction with anyone, we have a right to set that boundary. We can say "I'm not available for this", and act accordingly (sometimes by taking the conversation or interaction no further).

We must recognise and become familiar with what it feels like to have our boundaries crossed so we know in the future what and whom to avoid. It's also helpful to be ready to express when a boundary has been crossed without denying it (or denying our reality/experience) if anyone tries to cross it or shame us for it. This is why the phrase "I'm not available for this or that" is so helpful because many of us with low self-confidence find it hard to express our boundaries.

Feeling guilty for setting a boundary can be a sign of why we needed the boundary in the first place.

It's how you can keep your promises and accountability to the self. If you're not available for disrespect and available for respect, then you must be available for self-respect too, right? Look at what you're not available for and see how much of those you practise with yourself. The relationship with the self is the most important relationship of all.

This practice helps to build your foundation to secure and sustainable, upgraded self-confidence. It's an empowered base to live, work, play, and exist from.

Share with me on social media (@iona_barker_) what you like best about this practice, and I would love to know what you are available for and not available for, especially if you have anything that's not on the list above.

Chapter 7

Mirror Work

Mirror work involves looking at your reflection in a mirror regularly to say words of encouragement or affirmation. Simply smiling at yourself in the mirror can have a profound effect on the way you feel about yourself and your level of self-confidence.

You can look at yourself in the eyes or you can look at your body.

I love this exercise as it's helped me like myself again, after experiencing feelings of hate and disgust towards myself and my body in the past.

It's helped me feel confident about my body regardless of its shape and size.

The reasons you've been made to feel bad about the way you look can be to try to sell you products. Society has been led to believe external things and products will make us better because there's something we're lacking. Modern media and marketing lead us to believe we're not good enough just as we are. It can also be because the way we look (size, shape, height, skin, or hair colour) perhaps triggered someone else to feel bad about themselves, their fear, not being good enough, or poor self-concept (what they think of themselves).

We can't control how other people feel, nor would we want to. We've got enough to contend with without 8 billion other people being on our minds thank you very much.

What if you're good enough just as you are? What if the only reason you wanted to change an aspect of yourself was for the pure fun of doing it because it's something you always wanted to try, or for growth and expansion of your life experience?

A long time ago I decided to stop means-to-an-end living. I decided to stop going to the gym to lose weight or tone up, to stop working to just make money. Living for a result was keeping me out of my current moments. I had gone to school to get to college to get to university to get a job to get the house and the car to get to the gym to get the fit body and be conventionally "successful".

What was my definition of success anyway? Was it mine, or was I carrying around everyone else's ideas of success? When I checked in with myself, my definition of success was mostly made up of what other people wanted for me. It was based on doing and being to get and keep love or acceptance from other people. I had a thought in my mind "If I could just get that fit body, regular income, the car, and the business success, then I'd be acceptable to them, and then they'd want to know me and love me more". When I became aware of this perspective I was carrying, it didn't feel right to me. It wasn't my truth. It felt like I was chasing something that would never be enough. I was basing my whole life experience and goals on the possibility that someone else might accept me and want me if I did "right" in their eyes. An impossible task because everyone has their own opinions of what's right for them.

I tapped into a younger version of myself, my inner child, who never really felt good enough no matter what she did. If "she" was to get the fit body, grades, and academic success then "she'd" get the love and acceptance. Even though my university education was the most challenging thing I've ever had to do. At that time I was also in the gym every single day, obsessively maintaining my fitness and body shape. So that version of me worked hard to graduate and even got some work as a model. Then after that, the love and acceptance never really came, but the burn-out did. So I moved on to the next thing that might bring the love and acceptance that was craved so much. Then the next thing, and the next thing, always searching outside of myself for it.

Further exploration into this led me to realise the people I was so keen to get acceptance from rarely accepted themselves. How can someone who doesn't accept themselves accept me? They probably can't. I decided I was going to do things because I wanted to do them for me. No more doing things to get and keep something outside of myself. No more living means-to-an-end. I got good at assessing my decisions, (we'll talk about confident decision-making later). I still have responsibilities, and I still do things that sometimes I'd rather not do, but I'm slowly turning those things into a confident, joyful privilege.

I began to accept myself a little more, doing things like going to the gym from a secure "Let's go lift these weights because I like the way it makes me feel and I like to feel strong". Instead of being there feeling not good enough, comparing myself to the fitter humans, worrying that I was never going to "get there". Or thinking my body weight and shape were unacceptable through the eyes of others. That there's only striving to change and fit what society wants, finally becoming acceptable. That doesn't feel like freedom to me.

If we don't accept ourselves just as we are, then we're going to keep looking outside ourselves for that acceptance. We're rarely going to feel acceptable, lovable, or good enough in our now moments, and our now moments are all we ever have. Our whole life experience is made up of our smaller now moments all joined together.

Sometimes we obsess over things like our appearance, work, and making money as a distraction from the emotional pain of not feeling good enough, lovable, or acceptable deep down. You deserve to feel unconditionally lovable, good enough, and acceptable, and you deserve to have your now moments back. It's within those moments that we can be creative, enjoy other people's company, and experience real emotional freedom.

Let's do a little mirror work, and get to know and accept ourselves, so park yourself in front of a mirror (in private), and let's have some fun.

Start simply by looking into your eyes at yourself in the mirror and saying hello with a smile.

If you like, you can say things like "I'm okay", "I'm safe", "you're safe", "it's all good", or "Everything is working out for me".

At this moment, you're most likely safe, and okay, and you can find evidence that things generally do work out for you. If you don't feel safe where you currently are, these methods will only give temporary relief, (for immediate relief see chapter 11). Safety, stability, and security are basic human rights, including emotional safety and security.

I smile at parts of my body I struggle to like. I've noticed this helps my body confidence over time, and I've grown to love those parts of my body I once disliked. Will these parts of me change? Maybe they will, and maybe they won't. The point is, I accept them regardless. I'm not saying "Thighs, hips, and bottom, I will only love and accept you when you're skinny, slim, and toned". I'm saying "Thighs, hips, and bottom, I love and accept you right now, no matter what size you are".

This often feels uncomfortable to begin with, because we're conditioned from a young age to believe we're only acceptable and lovable if we look a certain way that's fashionable. Especially if we grew up with a parent who was critical of the way they looked, of our appearance, and criticised the appearance of others. I grew up in the 90s when it was fashionable to be very skinny. Looking at TV shows and movies of the time, body-shaming was common.

I think about all my friend's mums who went to Weight Watchers. About how the women around me were constantly battling their "weight" as if it was a cardinal sin to be heavier than what was deemed "acceptable".

All the fear of rejection, retaliation, ostracism, being unlovable, not enough, "too big", "too skinny", and the time and energy used up to fight, worry, and obsess over it all. When we could have been loving ourselves, and each other, and having fun.

I have some "bigger" friends, and the hurtful comments they receive regularly for what they look like affect their self-confidence. I empathise with the hurt they feel when I hear or see the things that are said to them. I love them and I think they're beautiful. I believe they're fully acceptable as human beings no matter what shape or size they are. I understand logically that the people who are hurtful towards them are, most of the time, projecting their fear and opinions of what they believe is acceptable. People who project their fears onto others are rarely happy within themselves.

When I see my friends standing in their power I think that's the epitome of sexy. It's an energetic thing, not a physical thing. For example, I can observe someone who is physically slim, what society and the media deem to be "attractive". Yet if they aren't in their power, they're closed off and discontent within themselves. They don't feel comfortable in their skin, and their self-doubt or insecurity is showing. It makes me want to run up to them with a big blanket to wrap them up and help them feel safe.

Then I see someone who's being their true self, fully in their body and power. They could be any shape and size, wearing anything, and it makes me want to shout "HECK YEAH!".

A decade ago, I wrote a list of affirmations that I'd say to myself in the mirror every day. At first, it felt weird and uncomfortable because I'd been brought up to believe that liking myself was conceited or narcissistic. The opposite is true: people who are conceited or narcissistic are generally insecure, unempathetic, full of shame, and tend to dislike themselves or have an unhealthy relationship with the self. These people go out their way to make others feel bad so they can feel good. They hoover up positivity and spit out animosity and criticism. The more I was getting to know myself and learning how to talk to myself in a kind and compassionate way, the more secure I was becoming within myself. The more content I am in my now moments. The time used to worry and fret about being good enough is now time to do more interesting and beneficial things, fun things.

Some phrases from my list of affirmations are:

I love and accept myself

I'm proud of myself.

I can feel confident in myself

I can believe in myself and my abilities

I can learn to love myself

I love and accept all parts of myself

I love myself unconditionally.

I take responsibility for myself and my actions.

If you struggle to believe these things, use the tools in this book to dig a little deeper as to why you can't believe it.

Questions:

- Was I ever made to feel unlovable, not good enough, ugly, bad, shameful, or wrong by others?
- Why do they get to decide what or who I am? Are they the overlord of the universe? Heck no! I get to decide what's true for me.
- If a friend or loved one were to tell me that someone had made them feel this way, what would I say to them to comfort and support them?
- What compassionate and loving things can I say to the parts of me that feel unlovable, unacceptable, or shameful?

Think of things that you might say to a loved one who may require words of affirmation from you.

Try creating your list of positive, kind, and compassionate things to say to yourself.

Journal about it, meditate on it, and ground yourself before you practise any affirmation.

If this practice is too challenging, then you may be carrying some internalised toxic shame. We'll discuss this later in the book.

Keep your promises to yourself.

If you say you like yourself in front of the mirror, are you keeping your word? Are you behaving in a way towards yourself that's kind and compassionate?

Many of us have self-confidence challenges in the first place because the words and actions of influential people in our lives didn't necessarily line up. What they did and said was conflicting and confusing. If you tell yourself that you love yourself, but then are criticising and mean to yourself, that's emotional abuse. Many of us have learned to gaslight ourselves or have observed others say one thing and do another. So, let's be self-accountable, and keep our words and our promises to ourselves by being kind and following through with our words and actions. Like the other previous processes, we're building a secure, solid foundation of self-respect, self-trust, inner knowingness, and empowerment: all aspects of authentic self-confidence.

In your journal or the notes on your phone, write a list of phrases like the ones I listed above that you would love to hear.

Questions:

- How would I like to feel every day?
- What can I say to myself to help me feel like that?
- If I could wave a magic wand and become immediately loveable and acceptable, what would that be like? How would that feel?

Can you imagine waving that magic wand in front of the mirror every day, and being immediately lovable and acceptable no matter how you look or how you feel about yourself in the moment?

Set a reminder on your phone for a few minutes every morning, to say these phrases and practice accepting yourself just as you are.

Sure, we all have things we're working on, but the world needs you right now just as you are. The world needs you as you are living in this moment right now, because the moment is all we ever have. It's time to practise a little self-compassion and acceptance so we can step into our authentic self-confidence. I believe authentic self-confidence is our birth right. What if there was a new human being who felt doubt about themselves, what would you say to them to comfort and support them? We set the standards, examples, and reference points for others with the way we refer to and speak to ourselves. It's time we upgraded our self-confidence, if not for ourselves, but for all the other human beings coming into this world. The world is a hard enough place for them, so let's be the relief, security, and softness they need and deserve. Let's give them what we perhaps didn't get.

Chapter 8

The Inner Child Toolkit

Trigger warning: There are mentions of alcoholism and suicide on pages 77-92 in this chapter.

Most of us can trace the origins of our low self-confidence back to childhood. The first causes of feeling challenged in our confidence could have been a life-shaking experience like loss, bullying, an accident, a medical procedure, or multiple experiences over time. Many of us experience self-confidence challenges because we're unable to process our challenging emotional experiences healthily. We learned to suppress our emotions because it wasn't safe to feel or express them.

Many human beings are living at the emotional age of when they first experienced their challenges. They were unable to emotionally digest and safely move through what happened in a healthy way.

Inner child work is a powerful way to jump-start our emotional maturity by feeling our feelings. To do this first we must create an environment where we are safe to feel our feelings. To feel is to heal.

Inner Child Letter

One of my favourite exercises in the inner child tool kit is the inner child letter.

On a piece of paper write a letter to your childhood self. Play with it at first and keep it light, to build up a relationship and trust with your childhood self. If they experienced bullying or were shamed in any way, it may take a little time, patience, and some back and forth to see the benefits of this exercise. That part of you may struggle to trust, but that's okay. You have the rest of your life to develop trust and a beautiful, loving relationship with the parts of yourself that need it.

Start by writing with your dominant hand:

Dear "your name",

How are you today? I'm looking forward to getting to know you.

What's your favourite colour? What do you like to eat? Do you have a favourite toy or game you like to play?

Lots of love,

"Your name"

We can use our non-dominant hand to reply from the perspective of the inner child parts of our consciousness. You may find it tricky to write, and that's what we want. Remember when you were learning to write, and it wasn't easy? Feeling our feelings isn't easy either. This exercise helps us access different, sometimes dormant parts of our brain, and to get into the mindset of our younger self. We're not reverting to being a child by doing this exercise. Our goal is to communicate with a part of us that's been hiding out of fear or hidden by others. Another goal of this exercise is to bolster a responsible, emotionally mature adult part of the self that takes charge and stands up for the hurt, or younger parts. With practice, this is the part that can step in and take over the running of our everyday lives. An authentically confident, emotionally mature, adult self.

Do this several times, and each time you reply to your younger self, say something kind and positive such as "I love that", "you're amazing", or "I'm so proud of you". This can feel contrary, cringe, or uncomfortable at first. A developing brain requires to be spoken to in this manner; all singing and all dancing. It also requires authenticity and sincerity, which will come with practice.

Ask your younger self how they're feeling, and always validate them. We do this by repeating back to them the feelings they've just told us, by being curious about it, and by letting them know we see how or why they feel this way. We're helping them feel seen and understood in their emotions, which is probably something they've rarely felt. They've most likely had their feelings denied or dismissed in the past. If the inner child says, "I feel sad", we can validate and be curious in our reply. For example, saying "You feel sad? Why do you feel sad?". Then we wait for a reply and go back and forth until we get an answer.

For example, "I'm sad because that lady shouted at me, and it upset me". We can then say something like "Oh no, that lady shouted at you, and it upset you? I can see why that would be upsetting, it didn't feel very nice did it?". Again, this can seem like a ridiculous way to speak to ourselves, but it's so vital for the parts of us that feel shame, not good enough, anger, and such. Any residual heavy emotions, unresolved trauma, or experiences from childhood or adolescence that happened when the brain was still developing. Seek out a qualified and experienced practitioner if you're struggling with this, especially if you begin to get overwhelmed with flashbacks, memories, or anything affecting your daily life. Make sure you find one that's trauma-informed, or has knowledge of childhood trauma, complex trauma, or CPTSD.

The goal is to create a safe space for your inner child to express to you how they feel. It's your job as your older self, to give them support, space, and validation around what and how they're feeling. We don't want to shut them down, minimise or dismiss them. This is harmful to the inner child. We don't want to use any invalidating phrases such as "you'll be fine", because in this moment the inner child isn't fine, and the moment is always all we ever have.

Practise comforting the inner child by imagining giving loving, kind affection. Human beings, especially children, need physical affection. Physical contact switches on certain parts of the brain, assists brain development, and helps to make chemicals that change our state of being from a threat or stress response to a stable and healthy presence.

Studies on attachment theory (5) show how powerful contact from a caregiver is in the development of the internal systems of a young person. Doing this exercise for a few minutes a day can help us mature and grow our emotional awareness. It also upgrades our authentic self-confidence. It can take a bit of time, but it's always worth it. The time and patience we give the inner child to see and hear how they feel will help develop their (our) self-confidence, maturing us mentally and emotionally.

Dismissing and denying emotions and experiences could be the reason for self-confidence challenges in the first place, so it's time to see, hear, validate, and have empathy for the younger parts of the self. They need to be loved and accepted in their feelings.

You may feel emotions coming up to the surface and you may feel the need to cry. This is normal, expected, and healthy. Crying is a powerful way to help us to process challenging memories or emotions. Let the inner child say and feel what they want. Validate them when they do. Remind them of how special, safe, loved, and protected they are no matter how they feel. You're their safe space now, and you're not going anywhere. You're going to be with them for the rest of their (your) life.

Inner Child Photo (My Exercise)

Note: I'll be referring to my inner child as "she" and "her" throughout this chapter.

I love using this exercise with my clients to transform self-confidence at the core of their being. Like the letter, it opens a healing and supportive dialogue with the inner child, who perhaps has never experienced one before.

This tool is best used with a photo of yourself as a young child from toddler to adolescence. Here are some photos of younger Iona that I use when personally doing this exercise. I'll take you through my challenging experiences that may have affected the development of my systems, mental and emotional health, and how I integrated each one using the inner child photo process.

This is me around 8 or 9 years old, and I'm standing in my Granny's front garden. Gardens and nature were always my sanctuary and I have lots of fond memories when I look at this photo. I loved my long hair, it was like a security blanket for me, but I hated it being in my face. So I had a colourful collection of headbands and scrunchies (many that were hand-made by me). I also loved my Sweater Shop jumpers and wore as much colour as I could because it helped me express myself when I didn't know how else to. I'm wearing a light blue headband and a bright pink sweater.

This was around the time I began becoming very shy and introverted. I had a particularly cruel teacher in school who'd pick on me in front of the class and call me names such as stupid and accuse me of not listening (I was undiagnosed ADHD). This affected my confidence.

I spent most weekends at my Granny's house. She was my dad's mum, and even though she was a stern woman, she humoured my wild stories and vivid imagination.

I believe all my grandparents on both sides had unresolved mental, emotional, and physical health challenges that were never integrated.

Not many of the post-war generation here in the UK (white, Christian, working to lower-middle-class) had knowledge or access to mental or emotional health services. Therapy and counselling were something that Americans did. Coaching wasn't even a concept except for in sports teams. All of my grandparents were negatively affected by the wars, austerity, rationing, gender norms, poverty, sexism, and being unable to process the trauma of the world in a healthy way. Even though extremely challenging, they didn't experience things like racism, immigration, colonisation, displacement, religious discrimination, incarceration, genocide, and other similar traumatic experiences that others around the world experienced and still do. The effects of their individual and collective traumatic experiences followed them through life. They were passed down genetically and epigenetically through the generations to you and me.

How could going through something so horrific, and being unable to process it in a healthy and supportive way not be damaging to the mental, emotional, and physical body?

Even though my granny's house was one of my favourite places to be, I was always worrying and felt like I had to prove myself, my goodness, and my worth to everyone around me. Everyone's love felt conditional. Granny could also be quite invalidating to my negative emotions, and I never really felt like I could cry or be upset around her, and most of the other people in my family. I was hyper-aware of how uncomfortable it made everyone. I now understand it was perhaps because no one knew how to hold space for my feelings or their feelings too. My granny seeing me in mine may have triggered a part of her that didn't feel safe. When I think of what it was like for her to grow up in 1920s Caithness, the highlands of Scotland, how challenging daily life must have been. They had no inside plumbing, running water, electricity, or central heating. Plus, with the trauma and grief of the First World War, I doubt she got the emotional validation and support she needed because they were all just trying to survive. I don't think anybody in that generation knew how to feel safe in their feelings. Everyone seemed to be avoiding, dismissing, denying, and pushing them down just to get by in life.

I believed I was a "difficult" child, and a "pest" for most of my childhood. I thought I had to be a "good girl" and do "good" to be loved and accepted. When I was with my granny she would often show me how to do things, like how to sew and use her hand-powered sewing machine. I'm so grateful to her for that, but also sad that my siblings and other family members didn't get the same treatment from her like I did. She didn't treat my other family members as kindly as she did me, and she could be quite cruel to my siblings and cousins. I didn't see it then, but I was her "favourite", and after she passed away, a part of me felt guilty for it.

When I started doing the inner child photo exercises and tapping into myself at age 8, I was confused about the world and my feelings. The world felt like a bad place to be in, but I felt safe when I was with her. At age 10 my granny exited this life, and I didn't have anyone to talk to about it. I couldn't even go to her funeral. I was in denial, and I completely dissociated (suppressed my feelings and numbed out). I didn't feel so safe anymore, and I think that had a lot to do with the challenges I experienced later in my teens and adolescence. I no longer had someone I could be myself around, so I shut my feelings off, learned to dissociate, and just pushed through like everyone else around me.

I didn't cry about or grieve my granny's death until I began this exercise because, before my counselling and coaching training, I didn't know how to. That 8-year-old girl could be happy again, smile widely, and wear colourful jumpers, long hair, and headbands.

When I began doing this process it was easy for me to love that 8-year-old. She was innocent, playful, and eager to please everyone around her. I found myself validating her thoughts and feelings more than anything else. I encouraged her to cry and express herself emotionally when she needed it, without shaming her. I would agree with her and could imagine holding her and comforting her in a safe, warm space full of love and compassion.

She didn't need to do or be anything to receive love from me, she was lovable no matter how she felt. Her sadness and feelings didn't make her less lovable, she's lovable because she exists. I didn't and don't need anything from her, and it's safe for her to just be. I created a safe space for her to exist and play in my imagination. When I felt triggered in my now moments, I took her there and made sure her emotional needs were and are being met by me, a very safe, loving, supportive, and secure adult.

This is me, age 13 standing at the bottom of my garden in my childhood home in Dumfries and Galloway. I like this picture because I stitched the flower on the centre of my top. I'm wearing my favourite comfy clothes, and very little colour, except for the small bright yellow flower that I added myself. It's almost like my true self trying is to come out.

My smile isn't as wide as it was in the other photo, and I look tired. I'm in my happy place in the garden, but this time was very challenging for me. I was confused and very lonely, and I didn't like myself very much. I struggled to make friends and was being bullied at this time. I began deliberately missing school and spending time out in nature if it was warm enough or locking myself in my bedroom which I had to myself by then. I would forge letters from my parents and hide in various places until both parents had left the house for the day. I was a mastermind at skipping school, and I went to great lengths to avoid it.

I often felt like a burden and began escaping into my art, drawing, sewing, writing, crafting, anything creative, and my imagination. It served me at the time, but what I needed was time and space to express and process my emotions healthily. Looking back I also needed support as I now recognise (I had professional diagnoses in recent years) I was experiencing symptoms of ADHD and ASD (autism). However, because I was the eldest I learned how to mask and look "normal", stay quiet, and power through. There was no support or even diagnosis in the 1990s for girls like me, because I wasn't causing a fuss in school. In school I internalised everything, and at home when I had a meltdown or struggled in some way it would be labelled as a tantrum or attention-seeking. I learned early on to keep my "fusses" to a minimum at home because I wanted an easy life. My parents would come down hard on anything labelled by them as misbehaviour. I was the eldest of my siblings and had to know better. It was my "role" to be the responsible one, and "the one they made all their mistakes with" (an actual quote from a parent). Though no one ever showed me what to do or how to be, it was just expected of me to know what was done.

My parents had another 2 children to take care of, plus their mental, emotional, and physical health challenges to deal with. The bare minimum was food on the table, which was more than many others had, so I felt I had to be grateful. I was often reminded that I should be grateful for what I got.

When I sat with this photo and this version of me, I experienced anger swelling within my being.

Both parents were experiencing major dysfunction in their relationship and their own lives and projecting it onto me and my siblings. They were separated but still living together in the same house, and it stayed like that for over a decade. This inner child version of me was angry at them for not getting help, and for not dealing with their emotional challenges. This child part of me was angry at how I was made to feel responsible for everyone else's emotional dysregulation, even though I was only a child.

Any self-confidence I had when I was younger was fading at this time, and I lived in fear. I was constantly worrying, expecting the worst, and I was often fighting with my parents and siblings. It was always my fault, and no one ever apologised. Yet I was constantly saying sorry or being made to say sorry. I was the one who was in the wrong, and I was expected to know better. The sadness I felt previously turned into anger, and I didn't know how to process or manage it, so I internalised it. I was holding confusing emotions and witnessing confusing situations. I had no one to help me manage or understand it all.

My adult self needed to make it right for that 13-year-old girl who felt angry, lost, and alone. When I began doing the inner child photo exercise with this version of me, I struggled because I didn't know how to handle her. What I was doing was seeing her through the eyes of my parents, and what I needed to do was see her through the eyes of me in the moment. When I did this I felt compassion and sadness for her.

I saw complex trauma (multiple, consistent traumatic events happening over a period of time), and thanks to my training, I knew how to transform it. The anger that she felt was due to constant emotional flashbacks, toxic shame, and intense self-doubt turning into self-hate.

She needed to be told that it was going to be alright, and she needed someone to have faith in her. She needed to be told she was fundamentally good at her core, that missing school and doing what she had to do didn't make her a bad person. She was doing what she could at the time to survive. It was never her responsibility to fix or manage everyone's moods and happiness, because she was a child. She didn't need to be or do anything to receive my love, affection, and acceptance. She was good enough regardless of how she felt or what she thought. These do not make up who she was, they're valid yet temporary.

We can find joy together and get the colour back into our lives. I remember reading a Rosie and Jim book to my baby sister at the time of this photo about a frog who swallowed all the colour in the world, and Rosie and Jim had to paint it back. Everything in life did feel grey and colourless. I love helping this version of me by painting the colour back into her life through compassion, unconditional love, and understanding. Every time I feel love for her, the colours seem a little brighter and more saturated.

Here I am, age 16, sitting in my friend's bedroom drinking alcohol before a night out. It was 2001, and I cut off all my hair as an act of rebellion. I associated my long hair with my childhood and I was done with childish things. I was ready to be an adult, and I was preparing to move away from home.

Home life was not a happy place for me to be at this time. My parents were still separated but living together. It was a toxic place to live, and everyone was fighting all the time. We had to move from my childhood home due to financial struggles. It affected both parents badly, who were still dealing with their own mental, emotional, and physical challenges.

I was so depressed but didn't know it, and the complex trauma symptoms (CPTSD) were causing much of my emotional issues. I had a strong urge to binge drink on the weekends to escape reality and gain relief. I also didn't realise I was heavily masking at that time. Everyone around me was experiencing so much dysregulation and drama that I didn't want to be a burden and cause further problems. Even though I was using jouralling, it wasn't enough on it's own. I was never happy, I rarely laughed, and I certainly wasn't

77

sad anymore. I was just at a level of numbness. I was internally shut off. I think about my friends at this time and how tough I must have been to be around.

I struggled in so many ways. Socially I had one or two friends, but outside of that, I could only socialise if I consumed alcohol. Thinking back, I don't think I was a very good friend. I don't think I was very kind, because I didn't know how to be.

When eating food, I could only eat certain things and I could never eat outside my own home. I was often eating things I didn't like and feeling unwell after eating. For example, I didn't like the texture or taste of meat, but I had to eat what I was given or go hungry. Plus being made to feel guilty for "wasting food" when so many others went without. When I was old enough to cook food for myself, I'd eat the same meal for months! I didn't want to appear ungrateful at a friend's house if I couldn't eat what they gave me. Most of the time I'd use the excuse that I already ate and ignore the pangs of hunger that followed. One of my best friend's mums was so kind and patient, and when I think back, I'm sure I could have told her I didn't want to eat the food, and she would have understood. I just didn't dare to do it, because at home that would have resulted in punishment.

Wearing clothes was stressful, my school uniform was particularly uncomfortable with the fabric it was made from. I had to cut all the labels off, and it made me feel nauseous when wearing it. I had a system for dressing and undressing, and a habit of wearing the same outfit for weeks at a time. I'd feel anxious when made to put it in the wash and be without it for a day or two. I lived in hoodies, big jumpers, leggings, and comfy cotton combat trousers. I felt ugly and tomboyish when I wanted to feel feminine and express myself with colour. There was no athleisure back then, and I often wore tracksuits that were far too short for me. I was already a 34" inside seam by the time I got to high school. Growing up in a small farm town meant I didn't have access to many clothing stores, and I didn't feel safe drawing attention to myself by wearing bright colours. I would apprehensively wear my favourite colours (orange, green, and yellow), but be watching my back. Someone always had a critical opinion, and it gave the school bullies & teachers more ammunition to single me out. If they saw me on the street or outside of school on the weekends, that would create drama in school the following days about what I had the nerve to wear and how much of a weirdo I was. I had to keep myself invisible, so I ditched the colour and just wore grey, khaki, or black.

I simultaneously felt like the problem and that it was up to me to find the solution. I constantly felt like I wasn't enough, but also lived in fear of being too much. I don't look happy at all in this photo. My posture is slouched and reflects how I feel about myself. I didn't like myself or my life, and I needed to hide because it wasn't safe to be myself. By the age of 16, there was no colour in my life, and I wore black and dark colours most of the time. I dyed my hair darker to blend in and be inconspicuous. I hung out with people who were blonde and "bubbly" who got attention, which I didn't want. It wasn't safe to be seen. This photo was taken just as I was about to leave school and go to college. I was convinced I'd be rejected. The uncertainty was causing me much anxiety and inner turmoil. My identity was made up of striving to gain other people's acceptance and at this time everything about me and my behaviour was deemed "unacceptable". I failed almost all subjects in school, and my attendance was so bad, even though I was trying my best to be a "good girl". I just pushed through because I didn't want to cause trouble. I was constantly very angry and confused at why life was so unfair. My parents compared me to Harry Enfield's comedy character "Kevin" and made a joke of my depression.

This was the pinnacle time of feeling like I didn't belong. The only emotional relief and self-confidence I found was when smoking cigarettes and drinking alcohol regularly. There were no drugs yet (they came later), but I had discovered using vices to self-soothe my emotional pain. I also found alcohol was a useful (and unhealthy) way for me to feel good about myself. It gave me a sense of fearlessness. I developed an alcohol dependency as a teenager when my brain and body hadn't finished developing fully. Getting lost in my creativity alone could no longer provide me relief from the emotional pain I was experiencing.

When I began using the photo for this exercise I was overwhelmed with sadness for the human I saw. She was trapped in a body and life that felt so awful all the time. I was sad nobody saw how much she was struggling, but I didn't realise how hard she was masking. Also angry that her feelings were passed off as a joke. To be honest with you, I'm still doing the work with this photo, and I find it challenging to integrate the parts of me that feel frightened of the world. It may take me years to do, but that's okay because I have time and I'm willing to spend it with this part of me. I want to.

When I ask her why "Why do you need to drink?", she says "It's helps me feel seen, safe, and confident. It also numbs the pain and helps me escape the shame it feels to be me". So, as my adult self I must do the work to help her feel seen, safe, and confident. She needs physical affection on her terms (like being asked if she needs a hug), words of affirmation, and reassurance that everything's going to be ok. She needs space to grieve her childhood home and the safety that was there. She needs support while she grieves the loss of her parent's relationship and the freedom of expression she felt in early childhood. She needs to know that she's fundamentally good at her core, even if she makes mistakes often.

It's safe for us to feel our feelings, and we're no longer going to shame, abandon, minimise, or reject how we feel.

It often feels strange to separate the younger self from ourselves. It sometimes helps to think of them as another person outside of us, because we can feel stronger compassion and love, and less shame. This younger human is worthy of time, attention, love, compassion, understanding, safety, security, and protection.

When I let my inner child be herself without judgement, I know her confidence is growing, and the need to drink alcohol to feel safe, seen, and confident becomes less and less.

Here I am during the most challenging time of my life. I'm 23 years old and living in London. So young! My clothes are colourless, but there still exists a pop of colour in my outfits occasionally. At this time, I was working in the design studio for an accessories company, and I enjoyed it. It only lasted 6 months though, as the team I was part of was let go due to cutbacks. This affected me so much because

I finally thought I'd found my place. I'm wearing grey and black still, but with a pink heart necklace that I recycled from waste items lying around the design studio. I was part of a team that was regularly given deadstock from the stockroom to upcycle into items to sell in the concession departments of the stores of London's Oxford Street. Much of my work was sold there at that time, and this felt amazing, even though I was only being paid minimum wage to do it. This was the first time I ever felt confident working as part of a group. The design team was made up of like-minded creative people and we all worked together to create amazing pieces, bouncing off one another, and helping each other to meet our deadlines.

I'm not a child in this photo, it's true, but I do include this in my inner child exercises because of the support I feel I need to give myself for what I experienced at this time. Also, the brain doesn't fully stop growing until we're in our late 20s. So chemically and neurologically I'm still developing my identity and the parts of my brain that make up my mental and emotional experiences. The parts that'll dictate my self-confidence.

To get to this point I'd made it through college and secured a place at a university in Glasgow to do fashion design with business studies.

I struggled all through university and felt that no matter how hard I worked, I could never be good enough. I re-sat failed exams every year and worked myself to the bone (I still have dreams about failing classes, missing whole semesters, and being in the exam hall). I was perpetually exhausted, getting sickness or flu bugs, crying, having meltdowns in private, binge-drinking, and chain-smoking. I remember working on my dissertation in my 4th and final year, going through about 40 cigarettes a day, maybe more. I was outside the library every five to ten minutes to cry, smoke, and have a meltdown. It was the only thing that helped manage my anxiety. I didn't know what anxiety was or that I had it. There was no talk of mental health or anxiety in my Scottish university in 2007. I got a 1st place (the highest grade) for my practical design work, but 3rd place (the lowest grade) for my dissertation and exams, which brought down my whole grade. I graduated with a 2:2 (the grades in Scotland go 1st, 2:1, 2:2, then 3rd). I felt disappointed but grateful it wasn't the lowest grade for all the work I'd put in, and very glad for it to be all over.

At age 37 I was diagnosed as neurodivergent (ADHD & Autism Spectrum Disorder), and I believe that if I'd been diagnosed at a younger age it would have made a huge difference to my self-confidence, and my time at school or university. Part of my journey is letting my younger self off the hook because she didn't know.

So many girls slipped through the cracks in the system, as our behaviour is very different from neurodivergent males. Young people diagnosed in childhood are now entitled to support, which wasn't available when I was growing up.

Going back to the photo, It's the year 2009 and I moved down to London to work in the fashion industry. I'd graduated 2 years previously, and while working full-time as a waitress (to pay off student debts), I set up my own clothing and costume business. The truth was, I was drinking, partying, and spending my money as a way to escape the frustration and exhaustion of university and what it took to graduate. I needed extra cash to survive. I had friends and work colleagues in the stage and theatre industries who knew I was skilled at sewing, so I started doing costume-making and repair jobs for them. I was still experiencing CPTSD symptoms and the full spectrum of ADHD and ASD. I also felt overwhelming disappointment that life wasn't going the way I wanted it to or was made to believe it would when I was little (just stick in at school, then go to college, then stick in at university, get a job, make some money, and then you'll be happy).

I still felt unacceptable and not good enough. I felt like all the things I'd been told about success, the things I'd worked hard to do and achieved meant nothing. I struggled to get a job in my field of study when I graduated, so I set up a side business while working full-time to pay my way, which was proving very challenging.

During my last year of university, I'd gotten myself into a toxic romantic relationship with a partner who had severe mental health problems. In hindsight, I see it's what I was available for at that time. He had a few similarities with family members in terms of personality. It's what I grew up with, so I thought that's what home and safety was. It wasn't. It was a way to distract myself, to sabotage my already failing university grades, because I had little to no boundaries. "Fixing" other people took the heat off me, my problems, and made me feel better about myself.

I had to prove my goodness somehow. I was burning myself out constantly, and there was always some drama happening. I believed it was my job to rescue other people and to sacrifice myself for others when the only person I needed to rescue was myself. The relationship ended badly. He'd been cheating on me for years with many different people, and whenever I found out about it he'd self-harm and threaten to take his own life.

One time after cheating on me with his ex at a party, he attempted to take his own life and ended up in the hospital. I'd never experienced anything like this before. He'd usually just say he'd made a huge mistake, and I'd always take him back because he'd convince me in some way or another. My self-worth was so low I didn't think I could do any better. He was an adult who needed professional help that I couldn't provide. Yet we stayed together because I thought I had an obligation to him and "us". While at home for Christmas in 2008, he called me to tell me he'd been seeing someone else for the last 6 months, and that it wasn't going to work out between him and me. He blamed me for everything wrong in his life, and stated this new person was what he needed to be better. I had so little self-respect and self-confidence, that I believed him and it affected me badly. I'd invested so much of myself in that relationship and sacrificed the little I had left of myself for him. I would drop everything and go running at the first sign of a problem, and I made myself into who he wanted me to be. When he broke up with me, I'd lost my identity completely and didn't know what to do. I felt used, discarded, and full of self-pity for a while, but then I quickly learned to supress it like I did with everything else that was tough. I'd have a big boozy blow-out with friends, shrug it off and move on without really coming to terms with it properly.

After learning about what had happened with the relationship, a friend of a friend offered me a room in their flat in London so I could get far away from it all. I took it without really thinking it through and got a transfer from the restaurant chain I worked at in Glasgow to one of their places near where I was staying in London. I set aside my little costume business and moved down with the belief this was going to be the start of my happy life and career.

It didn't take long for the stress and turmoil that I left in Glasgow to catch up with me there. Within months I was drinking regularly, and I was now mentally and emotionally quite unwell. The crux was when I began receiving demanding letters from companies about money that I owed. I could barely keep my head above water and was working all the hours in the day and night to pay my way. I could drink the stress away for free in the restaurants and pubs I worked in. This was the only thing that could keep me feeling in control and gain a facade of self-confidence. The owner of the pub was a functioning alcoholic and was supportive and enabling of my day drinking or drinking on shift. I was drinking to feel something, then drinking to feel nothing. There was always alcohol around, and it was so easy to dilute my pain and frustration this way, though it was always just short-term relief. My past experiences and pain could never be integrated in this unhealthy way using external means, certainly not through habitually using a substance. Though I didn't know this at the time. The next day I would always wake up with a hangover, and the fear, anxiety, depression, feelings of not good enough, shame, anger, and disappointment would be back ten-fold.

On my 7th or 8th month of being in London, I came home after a night out and was feeling a deep sense of despair that had been a low rumble for several years, except it was now a scream. Like the broken fridge that makes a rattle, it had turned into an overwhelming, jarring sound in my whole being that I could not shake or escape. I had piles of bills and threatening letters from companies and credit agencies that filled me with an unbearable feeling of guilt, shame, and helplessness. So, that night I wrote messages to my immediate family members saying I was sorry for the trouble I'd caused them, and ending my life was the only thing I could do to make everything ok. Part of it was indeed a last-ditch attempt to get their attention, but it was also really how I felt. I searched my flatmate's room for their prescription pain medication (I had poor boundaries, and they always kept a basket full of various medications). I took everything I could find, drank most of a bottle of vodka, and passed out on my bed.

I was very much ready to not exist anymore. The only option I had was to do the thing my ex had been threatening to do for years previously. I'd thought about it often up to that night, that I was too exhausted to go on. It didn't seem that I had any other options left. I begged the universe for a way out. I was out of money, I was out of energy, I felt overwhelmingly alone, and I had zero hope.

I'd spent months trying to figure out a way to survive, maybe I'd spent years trying to find a way to survive? It was hopeless, and I had a deep emotional pain in my being that was so severe, I needed to get out. I desperately needed my life to end.

I woke up early that morning and threw up all over my bedroom and the living room floor. I couldn't even drag myself to the bathroom in time, but once it was out of my system, in a delirious haze, I managed to clean it all up on my hands and knees with cloth and detergent spray, then went back to bed. Hoping that there was still something in my system and I wouldn't wake up in the morning. I prayed that I wouldn't wake up, I was begging for the relief of no longer facing my life anymore.

However, my body was able to fight it. After a very deep sleep, at around 11am, I woke up to my flatmate letting the police into my bedroom. Someone I messaged the night before had called the police on me. I felt so ashamed and very disappointed that it hadn't worked. The police (a man and a woman) stood at the bottom of my bed and asked me "Is everything okay?".

I said "Yes", and they left. My flatmate asked me "What did you do?". I said "Nothing", and it was never spoken of again. They must have known I'd taken all the medications from their stash, but it was never mentioned. I was angry and felt myself moving deeper into depression. I saw the flatmate again the following year and they looked at me with what felt like pity and a pinch of shame. I haven't seen or spoken to them since then.

The next day my dad drove all the way down to London from Dumfries and Galloway to get me. I felt like such a burden. The fact he had to spend all that money on petrol, taking time off work because of me felt devastating. These were exactly the feelings I was trying to avoid. I'm very grateful and thankful that he did that, though what I did that night was never talked about, ever. I think my mother told me it was a stupid thing to do via text, but I was never asked why I did it. No one helped me feel like my life was going to be okay, I think because they didn't or couldn't believe everything would be okay either, and it was so difficult for them to talk about. It became a dark family shame and secret.

I moved back to Glasgow soon after that, and back into the routine I left behind. I remember telling a few friends about what happened, and they seemed horrified. I took that as meaning they didn't want to know, so I internalised it and never spoke of it.

I started back in the same restaurant again and picked up my costume and alterations work. It wasn't until I met someone I was working with who was on antidepressants, that I even knew that was something I could try. So, I plucked up the courage and went to the doctors to tell them I might need to go on antidepressants. They obliged, and I ended up on numerous different kinds for over a decade. I'd need to change them often, because after a while they'd make me feel worse and suicidal again, or I'd begin to experience physical symptoms like migraines, grinding my teeth, and nausea. Turns out I was misdiagnosed. Another colleague I was working with in 2021 had ADHD. I began noticing similarities in our behaviour and habits. It was thanks to her guidance and support that I went to my GP to ask for an ADHD and autism test.

Looking back, I should have been treated sooner. I should have been treated the day after my suicide attempt. I should have been tested for ADHD and autism years before. (The word "should" is coming from my inner child who feels disappointed about being missed, overlooked, or ignored). What I really needed was support or guidance. I suppose I did a good job at keeping it quiet, because I thought that was what I was supposed to do. It wasn't safe to be seen, and it wasn't safe to be my authentic self. I'd cut off that part of me completely. What if I was shut away or had my freedom taken from me? I had a constant worry of "What if there was something seriously wrong with me?".

My confidence was based on my productivity and keeping a "happy face" at all times. I was bypassing my true feelings and experience. I felt so much shame in general all the time, so I learned to put a mask on. I wore the mask and buried myself in my work. In the years following I started multiple new businesses with the little confidence I had and used them to distract myself.

My nervous system was stuck in the flight response, overworking, and overdoing.

I jumped from relationship to relationship never really dealing with my feelings. I chose partners who liked me more than I liked them, but I saw myself as lucky and grateful for the attention because I didn't think I was worthy of anything better. I would string the relationship along until I finally plucked up the courage to quit, sometimes years into it. I chose unhealthy people because I didn't know healthy even existed. I always distracted myself with the drama and feelings of others. I put my all into a romantic relationship for a few years and feared confrontation (though I behaved emotionally immaturely and sometimes disrespectfully), feared being seen as my true self, and dreaded being rejected. My mental health would also cause strain on my relationships, and I'd push people away.

I began meeting healthier people, and it was a bit of a wake-up call. I started working on myself emotionally, becoming aware of the toxic life I'd been living, and all the dysfunction I was available for. I was being trained in counselling with my creative therapy business (one of the businesses I started when I moved back from London). I was working with people in addiction, domestic abuse, and trauma. I could see many parallels in my own life and began studying all I could find on the topics of trauma, addiction, neuroscience, attachment, CPTSD, and PTSD. My drinking became less and less, and I stopped using it as a crutch because I could see why I was using it in the first place. How could I support them if I wasn't better myself? That's hypocrisy and double standards which didn't feel good within the core of my being. I got myself into therapy, counselling, and some coaching, and found a system that worked for me. I found self-care, psychoeducation, and compassion for the parts of me that went through all that. I developed the systems and processes that I have in this book. I let myself feel the edges and deep spectrum of grief and emotions that I never could in the past. I gave myself time and space to process.

I dropped the expectations and pressure to be acceptable and good. I was able to manage the anxiety I'd grown up with, and the symptoms of complex trauma (CPTSD). I found a loving, mature relationship where I felt safe to be myself.

Suicide and suicidal ideation are extremely serious subjects. If you ever feel like you have thoughts of harming yourself or ending your own life, please speak to someone about it, as challenging as it may be. Preferably a professional who won't dismiss, ignore, or trigger feelings of shame. There are many free services available no matter where you are in the world. When experiencing something as serious as this, we can't just wave that magic wand for it to go away. We can't ignore it either. People usually don't just decide to unalive themselves (unless they've experienced a horrifying traumatic event) in a short period. Thoughts and feelings of this nature take years to brew and fester in our emotional and mental bodies. It takes time and work to heal and integrate the trauma of this experience, even the thoughts on their own. Suicide is never a rash decision, it's the result of chipping away at the self over time, as the inner pain and turmoil grows. It's often the very last resort when all other resources or attempts at living life have been exhausted. It's also something we don't just "get over" either. If it takes time to get to that stage of desperation for death, it takes time to gain back a desire for living. The trauma, stigma, and shame that surrounds it are lifted every time we talk about it openly. Even though it's a difficult subject to talk about, if we can create relief from the depth of emotional pain that humans go through when they think the best thing for the world is to no longer be in it, it's worth talking about. I also believe much stigma remains from suicide being illegal in the UK until the 1960s, and still is in many countries.

I have so much compassion and pride for the girl in the photo. We (she and I) are so resilient and tough, but we need softness and warmth. We need gentleness, kindness, compassion, and support. We need support in every way, someone to show us how to look after ourselves and be kind to ourselves.

That's our job now. We can take over from our parents and be the responsible adults that we needed in our lives. We're not doing it their way anymore, we're doing it our way. The fun, patient, loving, and compassionate way. That 8-year-old, 13-year-old, 16-year-old, and 23-year-old isn't alone anymore, and they never will be. We have access to authentic self-confidence because we can model it for them and show them the way. We can use the processes in this book together and grow together.

We can build a good foundation on some solid ground that we find and create ourselves.

I'm still working on these past parts of myself, and I probably will be forever. The more I work with these parts, the less they need my help because they've integrated. I've processed the pain in a healthy way that I couldn't before.

Maybe we'll always occasionally have something come up from unresolved childhood experiences, but I believe it'll be less and less in time. This exercise is a good way of asking questions that no one asked us at the time.

I want to be able to safely say "I'm not okay", or "That was a bit rubbish", without pushing it away or shaming it. I have to feel it and transform it because that's what it means to be healthy emotionally, mentally, and physically. I don't project, blame, or shame others for what I need to take responsibility for. Even though some of the challenging things I experienced were not my fault, I take full responsibility for them now. I'm the only one responsible for my being. This is what I know authentic self-confidence to be.

Inner Child Photo (Your Exercise)

Find a photo of your younger self and start with one that you feel little or no resistance towards. For example, I feel less resistance towards my 8-year-old photo than I do towards my 23-year-old photo. The ones we feel the most resistance or discomfort towards aren't the best ones to start with, because we want to start easy.

If you don't have access to a photo, you can also draw a picture of yourself at a young age. The drawing can be of any quality, it can even be a stick figure if your mind can recognize it as a younger you. This is why I always recommend using a photo: photos have more emotional energy around them.

Put your photo up somewhere you can see it regularly and begin a dialogue of affirming with them. Some things you can regularly say to the little human in the photo could be:

I'm so glad you were born
I'm always glad to see you
I love and accept you
All your feelings are safe with me
You're a good person
You don't need to be perfect to get my love and affection
You can make mistakes; I won't punish or abandon you if you do
You can have your preferences and tastes
I'm very proud of you
I love who you are, and I'm always doing my best to be by your side

You can use these when doing the inner child letter too.

This tool allows us to create a safe space to have compassion, patience, acceptance, warmth, and nurturement for our child self, who perhaps grew up feeling lonely, powerless, not good enough, ashamed, unworthy, or unlovable. As you do this exercise over time, you may want to replace the photo with older versions of yourself, from high school and adolescence. You will find every version of yourself appreciating the attention, care, and validation that you're giving them. This tool can be extremely powerful at creating the biggest leaps in your self-confidence.

It takes courage to see ourselves as who we are; beautiful, intelligent, special beings who just want to be. Beings who truly deserve to be seen, loved, and accepted. Integrating and becoming these aspects is where the power of our self-confidence upgrades is at its mightiest.

Chapter 9

The Inner Critic Toolkit

Do some challenging emotions and thoughts come up as you do the inner child photo exercise? Perhaps you struggle to say or believe some of the phrases I listed previously to tell the younger parts of you.

Relationship with ourselves are based on what was modelled to us by people around us when our systems were developing.

How we treat and talk to ourselves is how our caregivers speak/spoke to themselves, each other, and us. Every one of us has a voice that exists within a negative criticising voice, this is the inner critic. It's made up of every hurtful or negative thing that was either said to us or deduced by us because of what we did or didn't do growing up. Our mistakes, trauma, failures, and our toxic shame.

This would be a good opportunity to do some journalling, meditating, or some of the other processes in this book so far. Write and meditate on why it feels so tough, or why you struggle to believe some of the phrases that I listed on the previous page that we communicate to the inner child. See what comes up in your mind and body and write it down. Question it. Is this story, phrase, or belief your ultimate truth? Or is it something you've heard growing up? Was it projected onto you by others, or is it just something that the people around you say or believe? We tend to pick things up and they become part of our subconscious programming running in the background of our lives. Most of the time we're not even conscious of picking it up, especially if it's something that generations before us have said, believed, and told others. This is generational programming and trauma. It's time for us to re-write the programming and heal the trauma.

For example, beliefs around working hard, money, love, and relationships, beliefs that we're not the kind of people that can have or do a certain thing. Says who? If a parent, caregiver, or teacher told us a story about ourselves which we turned into a truth, can we decide something more beneficial? We perhaps took on what they said to keep us safe or because we didn't know otherwise. It's time to put down other people's stories and beliefs and create our own.

Can you think of how you observed a parent or caregiver speak to themselves and refer to themselves? Is this how you are too? Is this a beneficial way of being?

Our confidence challenges can come from the way we refer to and speak to ourselves. Self-deprecation is harmful to the being, and the best way to "stay grounded" is to have compassion and appreciation for the self. We can have compassion for the critical parts of us too. This doesn't mean that we let the negative and critical thoughts run away within us. When tapping into the inner critic most people see it as a protector. Giving this protector part compassion and appreciation can feel relieving, allowing the inner critic parts to lighten up, release their grip, and have less power over us.

Here are some techniques I've developed and used to soothe the inner critic dialogue. As always, I recommend you speak to a professional or someone you can open up to without fear of judgment if it gets too overwhelming, to help you gain some relief on the topic.

Inner Critic Night-Time Exercise

Our inner critic voice can be most active while we're trying to sleep.

To do this exercise, lie or sit down as if you're going to sleep or taking a nap. In your mind list out ten positive things that've happened that day or week. If you've had a particularly challenging day or week, you might want to think about good things that have happened in your month, year, or even the last decade if you're struggling.

These things can be simple pleasures and appreciations such as:

An enjoyable piece of music
A tasty meal or snack
A chat with a friend
A hug with your pet or child (Name your pet or child in your mind and imagine you hugging them or them hugging you)
The kindness of a stranger
A satisfying colour
The sound of bird song
A task accomplished
The comfort of your bed or chair
The coolness of your pillow or softness of your blanket

This exercise halts our critical thought and moves us into appreciation. Doing this instantly boosts our confidence. If practised over time, this state of appreciation will become more of a baseline for us, instead of the harsh inner judgement that keeps our self-confidence low. Not only will we feel more confident, but more content with our life experience too.

Inner Critic Thought-Stopping

The relationship we have with the self is the most important relationship we'll ever have.

Many of us were raised to talk badly to and about ourselves.

We've been culturally programmed to believe that self-deprecation is a sign of intelligence, when in fact it's detrimental to our overall well-being. An article by Elizabeth Plumptre (6) explains how we use self-deprecation when interacting with others to avoid appearing conceited, seeming more agreeable and less threatening. She quotes a 2016 paper by Rnic K, Dozois DJ, and Martin RA called Cognitive Distortions, Humour Styles, and Depression (7), which explains how constant use of self-deprecating humour can negatively affect our mental and emotional health by causing low self-esteem, anxiety, depression, and less general optimism about life.

Even though we use our sense of humour, and intellectually understand that we don't mean what we say, the nervous system doesn't. If you slap yourself and say it's a joke, your body's cells still react like they're in danger. It takes everything literally, so what we say to ourselves has a huge effect on our mental, emotional, and physical health, and our self-confidence.

Every time you say or think something mean about yourself it chips away at your confidence credit score.

As well as the self-deprecations, we all have the negative voice that exists within us; the voice that's made up of every negative or judgmental thing that was said to us, about us or we deduced from other people's behaviour towards us. This is the inner critic.

The inner critic can be incredibly shaming, abusive, and mean. A powerful antidote for this is thought-stopping.

We can use words like:
No!
Nope!
Stop!
Enough!
We're Not Doing It Like This Anymore!

Whenever we hear that inner voice chime in to put us down, we must become aware of it, and decide that it's not our truth.

Feeling emotional pain or discomfort when we have these inner critical thoughts is a sign they're not our truth. For example, if you make a mistake at work or school and call yourself "stupid" or "an idiot", this won't bring up pleasant feelings. If anything, it may cause you to spiral and feel worse. Is it fundamentally true that you're stupid? NO WAY! You're infinitely intelligent. The emotional body draws your attention to it by associating a negative feeling with it.

Observe the feeling without judgement, and once you've created awareness of the feeling and the voice of the inner critic, you can direct "NO!" or one of the other thought-stopping statements in your head towards these thoughts. How does doing this feel?

It takes time and patience, and you can always think of your now self as standing up for your inner child as you do it. You've got their back now.

Our self-confidence challenges may come from not knowing how to stick up for ourselves, and when we practise thought-stopping with our inner critic, it can help us to have the confidence and courage to say no, and stand up for ourselves in our external experiences too.

If you're not available for disrespect or bad behaviour yet accept it from yourself, then you're contributing to your low self-confidence, and you aren't keeping your word to yourself. This may also contribute to your lack of self-trust. How can you trust yourself if you're constantly putting yourself down? Instead, change it up; say something more positive or more supportive. Something to stop a downward spiral. If this feels challenging to do, start with something easy like "It's okay", "It's going to be okay", or "Everything's going to be okay". We're not dismissing or invalidating ourselves and our experience by saying this, and sometimes our inner self, (like our inner child) needs some words of support from our responsible adult self. Please note, if you experience symptoms of obsessive compulsive disorder (OCD) then please seek out an experienced, qualified practitioner to assist you.

You can practise thought-stopping if you feel your outer critic chime in too. Your outer critic makes a judgement of others. Try thought-stopping (in your head) when you're around others and notice how you feel. Everyone deserves respect, kindness, and acceptance. Many of us were raised to criticise others, and I like the saying that one finger that points to another is four others (of the hand) pointing back at the self. Meaning the judgement of others is a fear or judgement we have about ourselves.

If you were to explore the judgments and criticisms you have of others, what would that mean about you? What are you afraid of that you're projecting onto others?

Inner Critic Good Enough

Our inner critic can be loud and overwhelming when we're feeling not good enough around any aspect of our lives.

You may have been made to feel not good enough by your caregivers, teachers, partners, or people in your community. Or perhaps you were made to feel not good enough at a certain task or skill?

Sometimes, when we've been practising perfectionism, we find it hard to feel good enough about who we are and what we do. Or maybe we picked up the feeling of not being good enough from other people and society's expectations of us.

Who gets to decide that you're good enough? I believe that's your job.

I believe we can decide that we're good enough, regardless of our mistakes, or how we look, how much money we have in the bank, or whatever.

We can decide the only person who gets to "make us" feel anything about ourselves is us.

Seeking improvement in life and working on ourselves is great. However, I'm sure that where you are in life is good enough, and your inner critic's harsh judgement is unwarranted.

Decide that you're a good enough student, a good enough employee, a good enough parent, a good enough partner, and a good enough friend, even if you make mistakes and/or sometimes get it wrong.

If any of these still don't feel good enough, what action steps can you take to feel good enough in any aspect of life? Maybe it's not about doing or being anything different than you already are. What if you were good enough just as you are in this moment right now, regardless of what other people say, do, or what they want you to be?

We can't learn how to feel good enough from people who don't feel good enough themselves. That would be like learning to drive from someone who's never even sat in the driver's seat of a car before. For many of us, we're learning how to feel good enough for the first time, and we're the first people in our families to learn it too. What would it be like to live in the world if more people felt good enough about themselves and their abilities? Perhaps you'd like to journal or meditate on that question.

Feeling not good enough also contributes to feelings of inadequacy or imposter syndrome. We fear being found out as a fraud or a fake, fearing feeling unwanted, unlovable, rejected, shamed, or punished. This fear is deeply rooted in our primate brain because we're community-led, social animals at our core. In the wild, rejection was a huge risk for our lives. As children, we learn to cope and survive with any kind of treatment, because we don't have any other choice. We rely on our caregivers to keep us alive. We may have grown up with these feelings and stories of our not being good enough, but now we can question them.

What would be the worst thing that could happen if you were rejected by a person or a group of people? No doubt it would hurt and be unpleasant, but I believe rejection is redirection, and that we can indeed always find our tribe. Especially when we decide that we're worthy of finding like-minded people with mutual love and respect.

Questions:

- What would it be like to know and be surrounded by people who like and love me unconditionally no matter what I look like, what I do for a living, how much money I have in the bank, or the mistakes I made in the past?
- Does it feel like a relief?

If you have any negative feelings come up, this is an opportunity to explore why. You're lovable, good enough, and fun to be around. If you want to feel better, do better, or be better, that's great too. You can and you will. Right now, however, you're good and there's nothing necessarily "to do", or "to fix", apart from leaning into and calibrating to that idea.

Keep practising feeling good enough in your daily moments. It may help you to shift from being a human "doing" to a human "being". You exist and make decisions based on how good you feel instead of what you think you "should" do for approval, validation, or acceptance of others.

Chapter 10

Radical and Unconditional Self-Acceptance

This tool may be the most powerful of them all, and it is the one that so many people (including myself) struggle with the most.

Many of us hold internalised toxic shame, which is the belief that we're fundamentally flawed or wrong. We may feel this way because it was projected onto us by others. Or we feel this way because we made mistakes in the past and experienced challenging circumstances that we've not accepted or emotionally moved through healthily.

Our mistakes and flaws make it hard to accept ourselves, and we may punish ourselves for these mistakes throughout our whole lives. This creates our perpetual self-confidence challenges that stop us doing the things we want to do, being the human we want to be, or living the life we want to live.

What benefit does this have? Perhaps we believe it's keeping us "grounded"? Maybe we believe it's keeping us safe, protected from bad things (especially if we've experienced challenging things in the past), and keeping us where we're "supposed to be"? I hear a lot of people using the excuse that things don't work out because "they weren't supposed to". Well, I say, "EFF that!" You're supposed to do all the things you want to do. Your desires and dreams are within you for a reason, and the only thing that stops you isn't fate; it's your belief in yourselves and the belief that it's possible.

I believe that holding on to our mistakes and shame is keeping us small, stopping our dreams from coming true.

You might think if you radically and unconditionally accept yourself regardless of your flaws and mistakes, you might get a "big head", become "too big for your boots", have a "large ego", or be called out and humiliated in some way. Maybe this exact thing happened in the past, and your body's infinitely intelligent nervous system is attempting to keep you safe from future painful experiences. Self-belief is not the belief that you're better than others either.

When we accept ourselves, it has the opposite effect. We settle into ourselves, remember who we are, and feel authentic confidence for the first time in a very long time, maybe for the first time ever.

Radical and unconditional self-acceptance means saying "I accept myself regardless of my shortcomings, my mistakes, my failures, my flaws, and what other people think and say about me". It comes without conditions. We're not saying, "I only accept myself when I pass my exams, make that money, get that job, meet that person, do this thing, or have that thing". We're saying, "I accept myself with or without all of that".

It's radical because it goes against everything we've been taught to do, and like all new things, it takes time, practice, patience, messing it up, and consistency to see and feel the benefit of it.

It can be challenging especially if we have a lifetime of feeling unacceptable. Perhaps we didn't do as well in school, or we didn't live up to a family member's expectations of us.

Questions:

- Can I recognise that I may be putting unhealthy pressure on myself to be/do/get/protect?
- Is it beneficial to put unhealthy pressure on myself?
- In what kinder, more compassionate ways can I treat myself?
- What would it feel like to take myself off the hook for just a moment?

We sometimes believe we're only acceptable when we receive external validation from others. This is unsustainable and we'll never live a life for ourselves.

- What would it feel like if I waved that magic wand again and became acceptable suddenly, just as I am right now?

Is your brain and body fighting the concept because it's been programmed to believe that to be acceptable, you must be this way or another? Or you must do this thing or that? That you must not upset these people and you must be "good"?

I believe you're fundamentally good at your core. You were born good, and every human makes mistakes. We're mistake-making machines! Mistakes are our greatest learning opportunities. We can't go back into the past and change them, and it is not healthy or helpful to drag them into our present moments or project them into our future.

The best thing we can do is accept our mistake and ask:

- What would I do next time if there was a next time?

We're not shaming ourselves, or making ourselves bad, we're observing, processing, and learning. All the things that human beings do so well.

I want to congratulate you on your mistakes. This might sound confusing, but I believe our mistakes are gifts for us to re-calibrate and get back on the road of living and existing again. Our emotions are like a GPS telling us when we've gone off-route. Make a legal U-turn wherever you can and get back to your journey of exploration and adventure.

If we're available for self-respect and such, even if we don't necessarily like certain parts or aspects of ourselves, in accepting those parts we can feel relief around them. To dislike the self is to disempower the self. It keeps us restricted. No one ever soothed, empowered, or inspired by insulting, hating, demeaning, or abusing.

Accepting doesn't mean forgiving the abuse or misdoings of others. We're focused solely on the self. Accepting the self regardless of the things that have happened doesn't mean we have to forgive and forget or make it okay to have happened. We're not the things that others have said or done, or our past experiences. This is not our true self.

Can you accept your resistance? Can you see it as not a problem to be solved? Once we start playing with radical unconditional self-acceptance it can feel like a big exhale. I can accept there are parts of me I'd like to be different, and I can accept a person's behaviour makes me feel sad or bad (though I always get to decide how anything makes me feel). Once I accept it, it feels less of a struggle to transform my thoughts, feelings, and stories around. Once I radically and unconditionally accept myself, my authentic confidence becomes natural, because my insecurities and fears were coming from parts that I couldn't accept.

Self-acceptance felt like something I "wasn't supposed to do", because for so long I felt like parts of me were fundamentally bad or wrong, and major problems with who I was. Recently I've come to accept my neurodivergence, something I would have been shamed for a while ago. I can healthily shrug at my so-called flaws and "problems" because when it comes down to it they're not relevant to my success. Especially as I view the self and parts of the self with compassion, kindness, and respect.

Become the gentle observer of your thoughts and feelings. See when and where you reject yourself, or parts of yourself. How would it feel to accept that part unconditionally? In the next process, I share a practice I do when radically and unconditionally accepting parts of myself is especially challenging.

Chapter 11

Tapping (EFT)

In my coaching practice, I combine the perspective of accepting ourselves for who we are and where we are in life. I support my clients while they allow all their feelings no matter what has or has not happened in life. A technique I use to assist in the integration of all this sometimes-heavy stuff is tapping, also known as the emotional freedom technique (EFT).

This technique is especially helpful for anyone who has or is experiencing overwhelming feelings of shame or stress.

I do this when I've experienced a challenging circumstance, when I'm ready to move through a difficult feeling, and if I'm feeling anxious in any way. It gives me an instant confidence boost when I'm tapping while saying confidence-affirming words and phrases. I've used it for many years to integrate radical, unconditional self-acceptance into my body.

We can use tapping to create inner peace, and calm, increase our self-confidence, and soothe ourselves if we feel overwhelmed or in panic.

Tapping is so helpful because it gives the physical and mental body something to do so we can have space to feel our feelings. If you tend to overthink or get caught up in your thoughts when you're trying to feel, this process is going to help.

Let's try it. Find a quiet place where you're on your own. Take 5 minutes to play with this technique.

Using the tips of your fingers, we'll tap on points of the hand, head, face, and upper body with our eyes closed while saying a phrase out loud.

We do this until feelings become less intense, dissipate completely, or until we feel an internal shift in our emotional body. If you're new to identifying your feelings or you find it challenging, it may take some practice to notice the shift.

A good marker for knowing when you've made the shift is when you either stop crying or start crying. Even the sensation of needing to cry is a marker. I view crying personally as a positive thing for my body to do, and when I start crying, it usually means I'm processing emotions in a healthy way. It's taken me a while to shift feelings of shame or sadness when I cry. I associated these feelings with crying for a long time and had to practise the perspective that it was safe for me to cry. That it's healthy for me to cry, and that no one's going to come in and punish or shame me: I'm not available for that.

Let's use a number scale too, to assess where we are emotionally, and then see if we can reduce the number. On a scale of 0-10, 0 being the feeling is no longer there, or the story or belief is no longer relevant, and 10 being that it feels overwhelming.

Check in with your body and choose a topic you'd like to feel more radical acceptance around; something that will bring you relief. What number would you give it from 0-10? Make a note of the topic and the number.

Start at the soft pad of the side of the hand- the place where we would

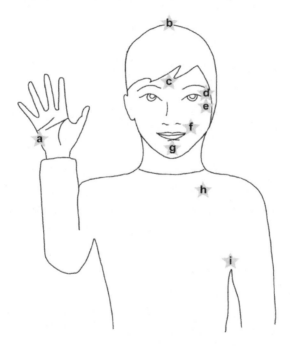

judo-chop (*a* on the diagram). Using one finger or a few fingers, we will very gently tap at a comfortable pace.

Take a nice deep, easy breath in and out and say this out loud:

"I radically and unconditionally love and accept myself", breathe in and out.

Next, we're going to move up to the centre of the top of the head (point *b*) and proclaim:

"I radically and unconditionally love and accept myself" and breathe.

Now tap in the middle of the forehead (*c*) and say out loud:

"I radically and unconditionally love and accept myself", take a nice easy breath.

Next, we move to the side of the eye: if you are left-handed tap next to the left eye, and if you are right then you will most likely go to the side of the right eye (*d*).

"I radically and unconditionally love and accept myself" and take a nice deep breath in and out.

Now try tapping underneath your eye on your cheekbone (*e*).

"I radically and unconditionally love and accept myself", breathe again.

How about we move to the space between the side of the top lip and the nose (*f*)?

"I radically and unconditionally love and accept myself", take a breath.

Now we tap the chin (*g*) and say:

"I radically and unconditionally love and accept myself" and keep breathing.

Next, we gently tap the collar bone (*h*) and voice the words:

"I radically and unconditionally love and accept myself", take a breath.

And on the opposite side of the body, we will now tap under our arm on our side (*i*) and say:

"I radically and unconditionally love and accept myself", and a nice deep breath in and out.

Then we tap back on the soft pad of the side of the hand again (*a*) and take an easy breath in and out with a sigh.

How do you feel? Let's go back to that topic and check in again, on a scale of 0-10 what number would you give it now?

The intention here is to lower the number each time. You may have to do this exercise multiple times to get the number to drastically reduce, depending on how much resistance you have towards the topic. Or how much emotion you're carrying towards it.

For example, you may be feeling at a 9 before starting, but then the number reduces to a 5 when you've completed the first round. Keep going as much as you like and as often as you can to integrate and embed your radical, unconditional love and acceptance. Especially if you're tapping about a subject that your physical and emotional body feels resistant around.

If you previously felt unlovable, unacceptable, or ashamed, you may have some resistance towards this exercise especially when saying it out loud. You may feel silly at first. This is normal and the best thing you can do is practice. You might also want to explore using the previous processes if you believe you're unacceptable or unlovable in any way.

You can use this technique for many challenging experiences that you face or have faced in the past. You can also teach it to others too and watch as their nervous system moves from dysregulation to regulation in a matter of moments. When we're tapping anxiety, shame, overwhelm, panic, or distress from our body, we must continue tapping around and repeating words until the feelings become less intense or until they dissipate completely.

For example, you could tap with the phrase:

"Even though I said that really silly thing in front of all those people I still love and accept myself". Or "I feel frightened to do that thing (exam, job interview, have that tough conversation, etc), but no matter what happens, I still love and accept myself".

If you feel a rush of emotions coming up or the need to cry, let yourself and keep tapping through it.

If you're struggling to love and accept yourself, would you love and accept another who was experiencing feelings or circumstances such as those you've experienced? Remember we're learning to trust ourselves, to keep our promises to ourselves by being accountable.

Chapter 12

Confident Decision-Making

If you struggle with self-confidence, then you most likely struggle to make decisions.

Perhaps you made decisions in the past that didn't turn out well. Or you were made to distrust your judgement by others?

The building and supporting of my self-trust were the product of years of keeping my word to myself, and the encouraging and compassionate dialogue I built between myself and the parts (many younger parts) of me that were afraid. It also came from the reassurance that when I'm acting in alignment with my values of love, kindness, respect, my truth, and knowing what I'm available and not available for, then I can't ever really get it wrong (though I can and do make mistakes, I don't need to be perfect). Even if I momentarily act out of alignment of my values, I can hold myself accountable and take responsibility.

I now know I can trust myself and my decisions, especially when I'm acting with integrity. I know there are people in the world who can't live the life they've been desperately trying to live; the round pegs trying to fit themselves into square holes. It's painful. I believe the emotional, mental, and sometimes physical pain we feel is because we're living out of alignment with our truth. It's because we're living in systems that are unnatural for us. We've been living in a paradigm that's keep us chasing our tails and distracted by our shortcomings. We also don't need to be perfect in our decision making, we can learn from the "mistakes" that happen.

How do we upgrade our decision-making? By getting to know ourselves, what we're available and not available for, developing our compassionate self-talk, and distinguishing whether the choice we need to make is any of the following:

Questions

- Am I doing what I think I "should" do?

Note that sometimes when we use the word "should", it can be coming from a wounded part of our inner child who perhaps isn't getting/hasn't had their needs met. Or feels they must be a certain way or do a certain thing to feel lovable and acceptable.

- Am I acting on impulse or to get a "quick fix" that will feel bad in the long run?
- Is it something someone else wants me to do that I don't have the energy or space for or want to do deep down?
- Is it something I believe will get me the desired outcome, and I'm only doing it for the outcome?

I've found when I ask myself these questions, I can get to a decision that feels better in my body. Healthier "Heck yes" or "Heck no" decisions.

It's also helpful to take time to make decisions. Sometimes we make decisions hastily to not keep people waiting or for the fear of missing out. The more I upgrade my self-confidence, the more I take the time I need. I'm considerate to the other parties involved, but usually, people are more than happy to give me a bit of time to think things through.

Making decisions and choices can feel unsafe, and many people would rather have their decisions made for them because it seems easier that way. Upgraded self-confidence means taking responsibility for our choices and actions because we're grounded and conscientious. I struggled to trust myself and my decision-making for a long time, but as I grew and evolved, my decision-making skills did too. As does my trust in myself and that I can't really get it wrong or mess it up. Especially if I'm making my decisions from a place of self-responsibility and authentic self-confidence.

How do you feel about making decisions? Check-in with any unease in your body. Can you accept that unease? Can you accept that making decisions was perhaps challenging for you in the past? For example, would you rather do what others wanted to do, or leave the decision-making up to others to avoid the pressure of getting it wrong? That it's not easy to trust yourself or your judgement? Now knowing what you know, how safe is it to make healthy decisions that are beneficial? You may want to practise saying:

I can trust myself
It's safe to make good decisions
It's safe to make healthy decisions
It's safe to make decisions that benefit my wellbeing
I don't need to be perfect
I'm getting to know myself
I know myself

Play with these phrases using the processes we've gone over so far. You're worthy of a healthy life that feels satisfying, and it may take a little time to learn to make the decisions we need to make to get us where we want to be. That's ok, have patience with yourself and accept where you are. If you're not happy with where you are, what decisions can you make right now that'll create relief for you?

Remember to practise what you're available for and ask for help when you need it.

Chapter 13

True Self/False Self

For many years I ran a regular free online coaching group that would meet regularly in a community setting to transform self-confidence. It was a great way for me to promote my work, practise my techniques, and create a community of growth in authentic self-confidence. I love to supporting humans in their mental and emotional health, providing hope and inspiration in a world that can feel dark and uncertain.

One of the best experiences ever is leaving someone knowing they feel better than they did before a session. This is always my intention, to uplift and inspire. It's what I needed growing up, and I feel it's required in the world more than ever right now.

The next process is one I was doing with my monthly confidence coaching groups, and I was always amazed by the answers they'd get. I've done this exercise dozens of times, and it's a fabulous tool for diving a little deeper into the self. To explore the most authentic version of yourself.

This exercise has two parts. The first part is to identify our true, authentically confident selves. The self that we perhaps used to be when we were little, and a self that we perhaps long for or wish we could be. The second part is to identify the false self which is the self we've created to help us feel loved, accepted, and safe in the world. This false self is made up of the roles that we've adopted or that have been projected onto us by others along our journey.

We're all born confident and in alignment with our true selves. The true self wants to express itself, and it's trying to get our attention. It uses negative emotions to draw our attention to something that's out of alignment with the true self. When we begin to view emotions as signposts we can look at them objectively and transform them. They're not bad or wrong. Yes, they feel bad, but for a reason. To get us to notice where we're out of alignment with the true self.

So many of us have un-integrated trauma around the rejection of our true selves. We've had to reject ourselves out of necessity for survival. Or our true selves have been rejected and made to feel wrong or bad by other people.

As a defence mechanism to keep us safe, our consciousness shut down the authentic self because it's not safe to be ourselves. It creates another self, the "false self", constructed using all the roles we've adopted to feel safe and accepted. Or roles other people expect us to play to be and do what they need in the world. That primate brain of ours is infinitely intelligent and is always in self-preservation mode. (Note this is not the same as split personality, multiple personality, or dissociative identity disorder. If you think you may be experiencing any of these, request assistance from an experienced and trained practitioner).

As children, most of us were freely able to express ourselves up to a certain age. However, if we were criticised, shamed, or made to feel bad about ourselves (How we look, money, creativity, etc) then the emotional guidance system presents a negative emotion. A red flag that what we've been told is going against our true self. That the outside perspective that's just been offered to us is not our truth, but at some level we believe it is. It hurts so we can recognise it and transform it (otherwise it wouldn't hurt).

An example would be an adult making us feel that we must behave "acceptably", and if we don't do it then we'll be denied emotionally nurturing connection. Which is the very thing that we need to survive. We may even be threatened with physical punishment or abandonment. (A parent saying to a child "If you don't come with me now I'll leave you behind"). This can build please and appease behaviours, unworthiness, abandonment/rejection fears, unlovability, or feeling not good enough from an early age. We then shut down the true self and exist from a version of the self that keeps itself hypervigilant for threats and acceptability to be safe. Where in life do you play "acceptable" (also known as the fawning trauma response), and is it in the same areas you'd like to experience more self-confidence?

Some people may have experienced regular abuse from a very young age. In which case I would highly recommend working with a practitioner (therapist/coach/counsellor) to integrate some of the deeply embedded experiences and programming. I like to remind my clients that the brain is very powerful. We can reprogram it with the right guidance, tools, compassion, and consistency no matter what we've experienced in the past. Your experiences and feelings are always valid and worthy of being heard no matter how hard they feel to express. It's also worth mentioning about medication and pharmaceuticals here. There's no shame in taking and using them to give us relief from our symptoms. Many are only designed to be used short-term (except from the types that are created to enhance longevity and quality of life). It's always worth doing the inner work when we're ready, so we don't become reliant on medication that's only supposed to be taken short-term to relieve symptoms.

Let's remember our true selves and recognise the roles we're playing, so we can feel more in alignment with our true selves freely and easily on a regular basis.

Grab a piece of paper and a pen or use a journal page.

On one page write down "My True Self," (you can write your name instead of "my") and on another page write "False Self".

I want you to think back to yourself as a child, around primary school age, tap-in and list the answers to these questions under your True Self heading:

Questions:

- What was I like before I had to be different, do certain things, or behave in certain ways to feel loved and accepted by others? (For example, outgoing, creative, passionate, fearless...)
- What was I like before I learned to judge and criticise myself? (For example, playful, silly, fun, always laughing...)
- What positive emotions did I feel regularly? (For example, joyful, relaxed, bold, optimistic, free...)
- What were my interests?
- If I could be anything in this life, what would I be?
- If I could feel any way in this life, how would I feel?
- If I could do anything in this life, what would I do?

Turn your page over to the False Self side

Think back to yourself as a child, tap-in and list the answers to these questions under your False Self heading:

- Who did I have to become to feel loved and accepted by others? (For example, quiet, well-behaved, good, mean, bitchy, or depressed...)

- What roles did I have to adopt to feel loved and accepted by others? (For example, people pleaser, parent's parent, scapegoat, a good student, golden child…)
- Ancestral roles: What roles do my parents or family members play that I know deep down does not serve them that I might have adopted too? (Remember observation without judgment), (For example, scarcity and lack, pessimism, fear…)
- Were there any people, actions, or things that depleted my energy and made me feel drained?
- If there's anything I could let go of or stop in this life what would it be?
- If there's anything that takes me out of alignment with my true self in this life, what is it?
- Are there any negative feelings that surface more than others that I'd like to have relief from?

Let's compare the two lists.

How do you feel when you tap into the True Self list? How do you feel when you tap into the False Self list? Notice that one feels light and the other feels heavy.

Take a deep breath in and out.

What can you recognise on the False Self side that's not yours? I want you to go down the list right now quickly, and ask every statement, feeling and perspective, "Is this my truth"? If not, put a line through it. Allow it to dissipate from your being- your mind, body, and emotions. Why would you carry someone else's baggage? It doesn't make you more worthy of love and acceptance; it makes you heavy and tired.

Your power is your perspective, and most of these are just perspectives. You can change your perspective. It's safe to change your mind and decide to no longer play a role.

Many of us become comfortable with these roles, they become part of our identity, and we feel safe. When we're receiving a level of acceptance from others, we're less likely to be vulnerable to threat or exposure. What if you let go of this role? Many of these roles have no boundaries, and we allow others to take our power away by existing in them. What are you available for? What is the worst-case scenario if you let go of this role? Will you be rejected? Unlovable? Abandoned? What must you believe is true about yourself to feel or think this? Is that the fundamental truth?

Look at the True Self side. What can you see on the True Self side that you'd like to integrate into your life now? Is this expressed version of you worthy of love and acceptance? What if you could let that true self back in a little? What if you could let that true self back in a lot? How does it feel?

Does it feel like confidence? Does life seem a little easier? Are we able to live in a world with more freedom and fun? Can you imagine a version of yourself where you're more of that true self? What are they like, what do they do, how do they act, and how do they feel?

Regardless of how other people act, many just want to be happy. If they don't, does that mean you still need to deny your happiness for their benefit or on their behalf? What good does that do? Those who would abandon or reject you for being your true self, do they practise healthy boundaries? Do they live as their true selves daily? Or are they living in their false self as a source of protection? Can you think about the roles they may have had to create throughout their lives to feel accepted?

In reality, playing a role doesn't do anyone any good long-term. Living in the false self may even prompt others to stay in theirs, and then no one is being their true selves.

The biggest gift we can give to others is to be ourselves. I believe our inner world creates our outer world. Our beliefs and perspectives all influence our actions, reactions, and interactions with the world.

The positive elements of the true self page are who you are. These aspects are part of your authentically confident self. Tapping into the good feelings and perspectives regularly can effectively upgrade self-confidence.

I recommend that you separate the two pages. If it feels cathartic to do so, destroy the False Self page, and with it any other negative thoughts, feelings, and perspectives. With the intention that as you rip it up or throw it away you're no longer subscribing to all the roles and heavy baggage that you once did.

Take the true self page (crossing out anything that isn't relevant) and tack it up on the mirror in your bathroom. When you brush your teeth twice daily, tap into the feelings and aspects that are on the list. Embody and feel into them. Assuming you brush your teeth in the morning and evening, this can set you up for the day ahead and for going to sleep. It also gives the mind something to do during the sometimes-mundane task of upkeeping oral hygiene. It's a good way to reprogram your software and get those neural pathways that make the connections of your preferred thoughts and feelings nice and strong. Remember that thoughts, feelings, and perspectives are like muscles. You must stretch and exercise them if you want them to feel good.

See this as a daily workout for your self-confidence muscles.

Chapter 14

Procrastination

Some say that procrastination is the thief of time.

I view procrastination as a tell, that we've got some underlying fear within our being, or we're burned out in some way. I also love to procrastinate!

I've learned to listen to my wants and needs on a moment-to-moment basis, and to manage my time in a way that feels best for me. I built my business with the intention of bringing inspiration and relief to millions of people, that it supports me financially, and gives me the freedom to live a fulfilling and fun life. It took me a bit of time and much re-writing of my programmed beliefs and stories to believe this was possible.

No matter what other people might say, I believe that it's possible. I'm the only one I need to convince.

As you might imagine, this threw up many core wounds and emotions, and my inner critic was having a field day. My inner child just wanted to love, be loved, have fun, and help other people do the same. I knew it was possible for others, so why not me? Who was I to think I could do it? The biggest challenge was believing it was possible for me.

This meant exploring my procrastination. I was constantly distracted by unimportant tasks that felt important at that moment, but weren't serving any purpose to my mission or moving me forward in the way I wanted, AKA busy work. I was putting things off and when I explored this I felt a sense of fear. Often, it was because I was carrying both fears of failure and fears of success, which created self-confidence challenges in myself and what I needed to do.

You may find yourself procrastinating often, and that's okay.

I developed a system for whenever I found myself not doing the ideal task that I set out to do (or was supposed to be doing). When the time came to complete this book, I found myself wallpapering my walk-in wardrobe, and I allowed myself with compassion and patience. As well as quickly observing and exploring my thoughts, feelings, and stories on the matter.

I view my days in energy more than time. Some days I have more energy than others. I'm naturally high in energy anyway, and I see my energy as infinite and powered by the universe at large. However, some days I get hit with what's called executive dysfunction and I can't do anything at all. This used to happen a lot when I was younger, and I was ashamed of it. I wasn't as productive as some of my classmates, and especially on weekends I would feel particularly burned out after a long week of taking demands and being a "human doing". My worth was very much tied to my productivity though, and staying in bed all day was a definite no-no. You might resonate with the shame and self-blame in procrastination. If you were to tap-in into this feeling, what would you find? Would there be an element of self-protection or a lack of safety in there somewhere? What else might you find?

You may not be in a situation where you have the luxury and privilege of designing your life and business to accommodate your thoughts, feelings, and needs as I could. For example, you could be a busy parent with a full-time job, or a student at school or university, or not be in a stable financial situation. Perhaps you're taking time off work for health reasons. Or you could be working a job, but you have an idea for another business or passion project but don't see when you'd have the time to do what you want to do.

Firstly, know that you can do exactly what it is you want to do, even if you don't know how the heck you're going to do it. I know how scary it feels when something you want to do is something that hasn't been done before by "someone like you" or even been done by anyone at all!

Set the intention that even if you don't know how you're going to get it done, it will happen. It's inevitable.

If you find yourself in a procrastination task (such as clearing out your cupboards), when you're meant to be doing the ideal task (the thing that you're procrastinating on), consider these:

Questions:

- What's more important or urgent for me to do right now?
- Is the ideal task time-sensitive?
- What task is going to bring more relief into my body? The procrastination task or the ideal task?
- If the ideal task will bring more relief long-term but cause short-term discomfort, is there anything I can do to make the task less painful and more pleasant? (Such as playing relaxing music while doing it, or asking someone for assistance?)
- Could I be self-sabotaging myself in some way because deep down I don't believe I can do it, am unworthy of it, or afraid of what completing the ideal task might bring?
- What would be the worst thing that might happen if I were to complete the ideal task right now?

- What could be the best thing that might happen if I were to complete the ideal task right now?
- Can I ask for help or assistance with the task from anyone?

Many of us who have self-confidence challenges also experience hyper-independence, but we can make more effective & efficient work when we call in others, and it can be lots of fun too.

- Do I need time to rest from the ideal task or time away from the ideal task? If the ideal task isn't time-sensitive, can I give myself a break from it and come back to it with "fresh eyes"?
- Do I let myself play?

(Many of us stop playing when we get older, but play is such an important asset in developing our cognitive functions, abilities, good mental health, and overall well-being.)

- What could be the worst thing to happen if I allowed myself an allocated time to play or do a procrastination task and then do my ideal task? (if it's not time-sensitive)
- What could be the best thing to happen if I allowed myself an allocated time to play or do a procrastination task and then do my ideal task? (if it's not time-sensitive)?
- Do I have a plan of action now? (note your plan of action could very well include resting, playing, or procrastinating if your task isn't time-sensitive and that feels more like relief right now).

Do you have more clarity on what you need to do now?

I'd often find myself on "couch lock", which is when my body is physically resistant to completing a task, or even getting up to walk in the general direction of it.

This would often happen if I had burned myself out, and my body was telling me it needed a break. I would also experience this when I was feeling fear.

Many times, I couldn't complete or even begin a task because the whole thing made me feel like a failure before I'd even begun. I'd be instantly afraid of potential rejection, retaliation, or aggression for saying or doing the wrong thing. I would feel fear of success too. The fear I would create something, and it would be too big to manage, that I'd lose my freedom and friends, and that I couldn't just have it work out. That it'd be too good to be true, and I would need to sacrifice something.

This was all coming from my childhood, the inner child parts of me and my programming from my upbringing, my beliefs around life, work, and relationships, and what was true for me.

I had to have a word with myself. Telling my younger self she has a right to express her experience and feelings. It also included swiftly telling my inner critic that "we're not doing it like that anymore", we're doing it my way, the kind way. The shaming, stigma, and invalidation of our mental and emotional health are the reasons we need to talk about it more. Those who are the most resistant to support are sometimes the ones who need it the most.

I can feel my body relax and my motivation return when I embed these words into my brain and being. Motivation is the opposite of procrastination after all.

I'd often find myself in a less physically resistant couch lock, where I could get up and do the thing, but I didn't necessarily feel like it. I came to notice that when this happened, and I leaned into it, had a day of reading or watching movies on the couch, allowing myself to revel in the peace and relaxation without punishing or shaming myself for not doing the thing, the next day or week I would find myself full of energy and eager to do the ideal task. It was as if my future self was telling my body to rest now because, in a few days, you're going to be full of beans. I would of course explore to see if there was any fear there, and most of the time it was very little or none. It was simply my body acknowledging the need for rest. The body is infinitely intelligent after all and learning to listen to it, hearing it, and not ignoring it offers great benefit to overall well-being.

If you find yourself on a couch lock (or bed lock) can you take yourself off the hook and allow your body to rest? If you need to complete an urgent ideal task, can you do a little bit of journalling around how you feel about it to see if there's any emotional or mental resistance that's manifested into physical resistance? Perhaps you do need a moment of rest, so can you do a short meditation or re-centring exercise to bring you the energy required to complete the task? There are lots of other processes I've talked about in this book that are useful, such as tapping.

For example, if you were to do a task and the outcome was not what you wanted, like completing an essay for school or college, can you still love and accept yourself? I remember experiencing a lot of resistance to doing my homework, schoolwork, and exams. I thought getting a less-than-perfect grade meant I was unacceptable, or bad.

When writing this chapter, I allowed myself to decorate my walk-in wardrobe. I enjoyed doing it, and I think it looks amazing. I allowed myself to rest when I needed to, and although I gave myself a deadline to get this book finished, I kept the pressure off, listening to my body for signs of when it was ready to rest and when it was good to work. Then I got back to the completion of this chapter feeling proud, excited, and happy that I let myself play as much as I did the things I needed to do.

I keep my promises to myself, always finishing tasks, unless it's a "no" from within my guidance system, and my energy/time can be used more effectively elsewhere.

Doing that fun creative task also gave me time to mull over the topic of the last chapter and how I was going to finish this book. It allowed me to just "be" for a while.

Procrastination eats away at self-confidence. Use some of the previous tools in this book to explore your procrastination if you face it and give yourself some much-deserved relief. You're doing amazing, no matter what you're doing.

Can you be a human "being" for just a moment?

Chapter 15

Movement

There are many other processes and tools I've used over the years to upgrade my self-confidence. The ones I've written about so far have been the ones that have helped me the most, but you may find ones of your own that are different.

I'm so excited for you to go off and develop your practices. I would love to know what ones you find and how they've worked for you.

I know that many people use yoga, dance, exercise, and things like tai chi and qi gong in their practices. I love to exercise, and I use this as a confidence practice in a way that I put on some uplifting music and head to the gym. While moving my body, I visualise my most authentically confident, true self and use the music to tap into my feelings of freedom, relief, fun, excitement, empowerment, satisfaction, and anything else that I want to embody that feels good.

I also love swimming and have done it since I was little. I love to float on my back and imagine the way I'm being supported by the water is the way that the universe supports me; it's easy and I don't need to do anything except follow my inner guidance. I can tap into bliss when I'm floating in the pool, especially when the warm sun hits the water through the window (and pretend I'm floating in the warm ocean or a tropical pool). The support is effortless and unconditional, meaning I'm supported even if I'm not in a particularly good mood that day. How I'm feeling is irrelevant: I'm always supported just because I am. It's sometimes helpful to remember I don't need to do it all, that there's some unseen force that's supporting me too, and that it's safe for me to take my foot off the gas pedal sometimes.

You may call this unseen force Source energy, God, angels, the universe, consciousness, karma, Buddha, Jesus, Allah, your guides, your ancestors, it's all acceptable. As I said at the start, I don't believe there is an angry bearded man up in the clouds judging us, but I do believe there's a universal mechanism of consciousness that reflects back to us what we fundamentally believe to be true. A consciousness that uses love and compassion as a building block or tool to create life.

I don't know much about yoga apart from that it's been used for millennia to bring us back into our bodies, minds, and spirits. I have many friends who swear by yoga, and I love to hear them talk about it and see how much it benefits their own lives. My yoga practice is simply one of regular stretching. I don't know any of the names of the poses I do, but I know that my body always feels more grounded and confident as I stand a little taller and feel into the stretch of my body. I need to do it consciously and carefully though as I experience hyper-mobility, which is where the joints in the body can over-stretch and be overstimulated causing pain and inflammation.

Many years ago, I taught and experimented with qi gong, a type of movement meditation. I loved it and still do it on occasion. Paired with visualisations, it can be very powerful for pulling our energy back into the body. I always stood a little taller even after just five minutes of practice. Qi gong is very similar to tai chi, but with qi gong, you're often standing on the spot. Tai chi involves more movement and is a slowed-down form of martial art.

I love being open to new things, and I believe that's one of the positive side-effects of this work. I feel confident and safe to try new things. If it doesn't work out, that's okay, there are almost always aspects I can learn and take from it. Having said that, not everything needs to be a lesson. We can explore and play for the sheer fun of it.

One thing I want to try again is dancing. I loved to dance as a child and attended a weekly dance class on a Saturday from the age of 3 to 11. I would also take part in community dance shows in my local town hall. Tap dancing was my ultimate favourite, and you could often find me click-clacking away in the kitchen throughout my childhood. It was noisy and a little obnoxious but loads of fun.

As I got older and less confident, I became closed off and hyper-aware of my actions around others. It was no longer safe for me to express myself, and I felt dancing was drawing unwanted attention to me. I had another negative experience in my 20's which put me off completely. I rarely danced in public, and only ever danced socially if I was under the influence of alcohol.

I will however dance if I'm on my own at home and listening to good music. I love the feeling of listening to the beat and allowing my body to move in time with it. Sometimes it's simply nodding my head or tapping my feet, and other times I'm hurling myself around the room re-enacting popular dance movies of the 1980s.

Many of us who've lived with self-confidence challenges experienced trauma in the past and popped out of our physical bodies, and up into our heads, where we spend most of our time. The amazing thing about movement is it brings us back down into our bodies. Coupled with other modalities and practices, we can feel safe to exist in the physical body again. Our consciousness naturally exists in coherence across our mind, physical body, and emotions. However due to traumatic experiences, whether one-off or consistent trauma such as abuse, we compartmentalise and switch off important parts for survival. Coming back into a state of coherence is a powerful tool for upgraded self-confidence and greater well-being.

Emotion means energy in motion, so using movement or motion to work through and process our challenging feelings and experiences can be of great benefit and advantage. Energy wants to move, and the relief we can feel from using movement, even walking, can be the cherry on the cake of our upgraded authentic self-confidence.

What's your favourite way to move? How does it help you feel?

Chapter 16

I'm All Processed-Out!

A while ago I was doing lots of daily processes, reading lots of books about building habits, and all the things that so-called "successful" people do every day.

At one point I got "all processed-out", and decided the most important things I could do every day were to exist and integrate all the profound shifts I'd made. Not getting too bogged down by processes.

Nowadays I only really whip out these processes in the moments I need them. I regularly use my journal when I feel I can work through a challenging situation on my own. I love feeling the emotional and mental shifts (it's taken me years of practise), where I give myself and my inner child a good pep-talk. I use my light grounding visualisation almost every day because it's fun to do at the moment and it brings me profound feelings of joy and bliss. I use tapping (EFT) when I find myself stressed and overwhelmed in the moment, and I regularly check in on my inner child. These practices have become second nature now.

I still experience challenges, but my upgraded self-confidence assists me in doing what I need to do and being who I want to be. I won't be dancing down the street any time soon, or jumping on stage to sing, dance, or act in front of hundreds of people, that's just not who I am. If that's who you are, then amazing! I hope this book has helped you be more you.

You may not necessarily relate to my own experiences, but I hope reading them has helped give you some confidence to share your own. Your experiences are valid.

Yes, we must put in work if we want to see and become the person we truly want and deserve to be, but I believe we're here to usher in a new paradigm of living.

I don't want to spend my whole life working like my ancestors did, especially as the retirement age goes up every year!

My most valuable commodities on this earth are my time and my energy, and I plan on spending them well. In peace and harmony with Mother Earth, with my fellow humans, and with joy, excitement, satisfaction, adventure, and exploration of our outer and inner world.

I believe we're all worthy of abundance, safety, security, health, love, peace, and joy simply because we exist. It's our human right to have access to all these things, with no exceptions.

If you're reading your first pass through this book, then I urge you to pick up a notebook and pen and begin the work: there is no better time than now. If you can't do it right now, then set a time and a day in your diary or phone every day to do some. The world needs your stories, your hope, and your life experience more than ever. The revelations you'll discover may give you just what you've been looking for, and you may not realise how much you can positively influence others around you. Remember that everything you need is within you.

I hope you'll find me online and drop me a message to say hi and let me know how you're getting on. I'd love to hear about the changes you've seen and felt since you started your self-confidence upgrades.

I would love to know any nuggets or "Eureka!" moments that you had while using any of these processes.

All these tools are designed for you to work on your own as self-help. However, I believe that co-help can be just as important as self-help. The most important factor of co-help is that we're not judged or made bad for sharing our experiences or how we feel. Co-help is a powerful tool for transforming our self-confidence.

As well as using the tools and exercises in this book, set an intention to find a human whom you trust and feel safe to open up to. If this is new and feels like a scary concept, reach out to a trusted human in your school, college, place of work, or doctor, who will be able to direct you towards a service to use. You can always do an online search too, for services that may be suitable for your circumstances.

Many with self-confidence challenges have experienced relational trauma. It's in our relationships with safe and secure humans that we may find our greatest healing and transformations.

This work is yours to do, no one else is going to come in do it for you. It would be unfair to expect or ask others to do that.

The reason you may experience self-confidence challenges is not your fault, but it's your responsibility to work on it and transform it.

One of the amazing things I love about this work and the tools in this book is how much we can influence other people around us. When our friends and family witness the growth in us, it can help them to know it is possible, and even help them to feel safer within themselves, and to trust themselves.

It's also true that our growth can intimidate others too, and they may try to bring us down. Are we available for that? Are we so powerless that we let other people dictate how we feel, what we do, and who we are as humans? This may have been a yes answer for so many of us in the past, but now we know otherwise. We know that when others see us in our power and they have a problem with it, it rarely has anything to do with us. It has to do with where they are emotionally. Our authentic self-confidence could be triggering a perceived lack or fear within their being. Maybe their inner child needs some love and acceptance, and at the end of the day, they're the only ones who can give it to their inner child. Just like we're the only ones who can give it to ours.

We can never convince or force people of anything. The best we can ever only do is practice being our true, authentic, peaceful, coherent, confident selves. When we become our most authentically confident selves, we become an energetic match to others who are more compatible with us. Relationships become more joyful and fun, and those who cause us stress and strife can fall away. We always need to do the boundary checks too, no one has the right to be disrespectful no matter who they are.

I encourage you to pass a copy of this book on to those people in your life who may be struggling with confidence. There may be many more people than you realise.

Remember that the work of upgrading your self-confidence can take time and consistency, so have patience, compassion, and kindness with yourself, and keep showing up for yourself.

I believe in you.

Loads of love,

Iona x

Upgrade your Self-Confidence

References

1. https://www.ncbi.nlm.nih.gov/pmc/articles/PMC3505408/

2. https://www.forbes.com/health/mind/benefits-of-meditation/

3.https://www.verywellmind.com/what-is-earthing-5220089#:~:text=May%20Improve%20Chronic%20Fatigue%20and,depression%2C%20stress%2C%20and%20pain.

4. https://www.ncbi.nlm.nih.gov/pmc/articles/PMC4401823/

5. https://www.simplypsychology.org/attachment.html

6.https://www.verywellmind.com/what-is-self-deprecation-5186918

7. https://www.ncbi.nlm.nih.gov/pmc/articles/PMC4991044/

Printed in Great Britain
by Amazon

38449806R00096